The Vice President

The Electronic Transfer

VOLUME II

The Death Trap

CAROLINADEIVID

"OUR VERY FREEDOM CAME UNDER ATTACK"

Terrorists destroy the fabric of any society and everything we stand for. Terrorist acts can never be tolerated or taken lightly but we need a fair and just society as well. The challenge is to find the balance. A system that upholds everyone's rights whilst safeguarding the lives and freedoms of our valuable citizens.

NEVERTHELESS
Guantanamo Bay Cages are based on an idea by a 16th Century English 'jack of all trades' called Christopher Wren. He was an anatomist, astronomer, geometer, mathematician-physicist, the highly acclaimed architect, a surveyor, an inventor of intravenous injection, an anatomical illustrator or a brain imaging artist, a medical dissector and a trend-setter. It is true he was great, but this was in the 1650s. To be precise, his Colony Collapse Studies behind the modern-day equivalent Guantanamo Bay Cages were carried out in 1654. Do you also know that slavery was being introduced in North America at the same time? A court in North America, Virginia in 1654 in Anthony Johnson v Robert Parker the court made a ground-breaking judgment that free blacks can own other blacks as slaves? Yet in 2002 we are still using the same ideas to hold people indefinitely.
We need to move with the times.
SET FREE!
CLOSE GUANTANAMO BAY CAGES.

DEDICATION

Mankind over the centuries has played God maintaining the ecological balance through wars. Mankind has evolved and we are entering another phase of development where networking and cooperation are the norms. Instead of cutting defense and military budget in line with this great achievement we are still spending $trillions on weapons. It's either we reduce the defense budget and use it on other sectors to maintain ecological balance or face the extinction of mankind. Small friction can trigger a Nuclear World War that will result in the extinction of mankind. But nevertheless, can this give a few evil people the right to loot all banks and all the money in the economy to make Weapons of Mass Destruction? Their aim; to play God and set a time-bomb that will kill more than half to two-thirds of the population. Who has a right to make WMDs? Are you going to just stand and watch? Putting your life in someone's hands? Why can't we just convince these leaders that aliens don't exist and as such we don't see why we keep on making weapons when all the world is becoming One? Fostering superior thinking the only way forward.

ACKNOWLEDGMENTS

A big thanks to Touchladybirdlucky Studios and best wishes to the Carolinadeivid Brand.

Carolinadeivid

CHAPTER ONE

THE DEATH TRAP

This Volume relies on a fictional film Script which I wrote called:
9/11 The Death Trap but one based on facts that will help debunk
the conspiracy theories regarding the 9/11 attacks, the impact,
and the aftermath.
In my script, the setting is London 1600s replayed in New York
USA from 2001.
The Actors:
Christopher Wren (1632-1673) is played by Larry Silverstein
King Charles II (1630-1685) is played by President George W.
Bush.
Mayor Thomas Bloodworth (1620-1682) is played by Mayor Rudy
Giuliani the Mayor of Newyork.
Samuel Pepys (1633-1703) is played by the Secretary of Defense
Donald Rumsfeld.
Setting: England from 1654.
A Christopher Wren, an English anatomist, astronomer, geometer,
mathematician-physicist, the highly acclaimed architect, a
surveyor, an inventor of intravenous injection, an anatomical
illustrator and a trend-setter [Wikipedia] embarked on a
groundbreaking challenge to carry out experiments, observations
and to record everything into manuals. His observational studies
and experiments were carried out to find the best methods, best
designs, best standards and best ways of doing things. He aimed
to find answers to problems of his day from architecture to
medicine. Throughout his life he was very active, writing articles,
devising methods and writing down results drawn from his

experiments. His first studies relevant to this report were the Colony (Society) Collapse Studies. He designed a transparent design that was octagonal with three zones for holding worker-bees in captivity indefinitely. The idea was to study the impacts of putting male worker-bees into captivity and the impact that has on the remaining colony. The transparent container had glasses so that observers could see and study the bees. This transparent 3 story containment made of glass became the basic blueprint for the World Trade Center Plans. Just like Christopher Wren's transparent Colony Collapse Observational container the World Trade Center had three zones. There was one express-elevator that linked all three zones just like with Wren's design even though local elevators were present too, a single passage connected all the stories (zones). The World Trade Center Buildings incorporated the idea of transparency as well through the use of the rib vaulting and buttresses columns with glasses. Just like Christopher Wren's design, the idea was to trap the bees so that they remain inside and make honey inside. The design of the World Trade Center made the buildings a Death Trap. The points where the airplanes struck the towers were the critical points for any escape route. The impact of the planes exactly where they impacted created an automatic Death Trap. The points were the critical exit points for the escape route of the people from the buildings through the express elevators. The towers became Death Traps and someone 'within' knew this and this information was way out of reach of the terrorists. 9/11 attacks were a cold and calculated highly sophisticated mass murder plan beyond the capabilities of terrorists. After the destruction of the World Trade Center Towers Christopher Wren's Colony (Society) Collapse Studies' idea was further adopted again and used to create the Guantanamo Bay Cages. We know for sure that this Christopher Wren was the inventor of intravenous injection experimenting with dogs injecting opium into their bloodstream. We also know how deranged he was at one point suggesting that blood inside animals could be replaced with ale, opium or wine. We also know that he was obsessed with the functions of the brain and in brain imaging in neurology. Christopher Wren also "produced drawings for Thomas Willis's 1664 book Cerebri Anatome (The Anatomy of the Brain). This was a landmark publication in the history of neurology, not least because of Wren's detailed and accurate figures, which were among the very first modern images of brain anatomy." [History of Surgery and Anesthesia]

Have you seen the link now?

To study the brain, blood and human body this Christopher Wren first discovered a way of having cheap subjects (guinea pigs) to experiment on. He can't carry out experiments on free humans. He had to find a way of abusing them holding them against their will, hence the modern equivalents of the transparent enclosures Auschwitz and Guantanamo Bay Cages. Although the idea was initially for bees, I think he later moved to humans as we see him now studying the brain's imaging with astonishing accuracy.

This Christopher Wren could also be the very man who might have influenced and or behind the Auschwitz concentration camps. The only question not answered here is this. What is the government's real motive behind the Guantanamo Bay Cages? Christopher Wren was a member of the Royal Exchange; the first scientific observational center. Here he learned about astronomy, inventing and correcting telescopes, studying the effects of gravity, the impact of gunpowder as a demolition propellant, the use of a plummet, the use of a battering ram for demolition. Years later before and after the Great Fire of London of 1666, he became the King's Surveyor designing the whole city of London. It is his blueprints which were also used to design Newyork and it is a fact that Newyork is a sister city of London based on the work of this man.

All his work has been documented to the extent that he has answers to every problem before and after the 9/11 attacks. It seemed someone opened his manuals and prescribed the same solutions to Newyork and the USA's problems pre-9/11. The only question is who and why? Hence my film script: The Death Trap. Do you also know that he invented the idea of Cycloids a method that can be used to predict the fall of stock markets? His method predicted the financial crisis giving the exact time this was going to happen. See calculations under cycloids. This same method predicted the rise to power as the President of the United States of a tan-gentleman (Tangent)? Barack Obama in 2009? This scientist was "on fire" during his days no wonder why he influenced every aspect of human history.

Fasten your seatbelts because what you are going to read will shock the hell out of you.

Sometimes you must know the past to explain the present and the future!

Script Writer
Carolinadeivid Copyright © 2019 Carolinadeivid All rights reserved.
The Death Trap!

UNDERLYING PRINCIPLES

Mirror-Image Something that looks the same as another thing but with its left and right sides in an opposite direction. (reflected image) [Cambridge Dictionary].
Self-fulfillment Prophecy This is a prediction that itself becomes true direct or indirectly because the person who made the prediction will act on it so that it is realized in the end. This is a prophecy that is less truthful at the time of prediction but one that influences people to change their behavior that in the end, it becomes real.
Film Director A film director is a person who directs the making of a film. A film director controls a film's artistic and dramatic aspects and visualizes the screenplay (or script) while guiding the technical crew and actors in the fulfillment of that vision. The director has a key role in choosing the cast members, production design and the creative aspects of film-making.[1] Under European Union law, the director is viewed as the author of the film. [Wikipedia]
Prophet In religion, a prophet is an individual who is regarded as being in contact with a divine being and is said to speak on that entity's behalf, serving as an intermediary with humanity by delivering messages or teachings from the supernatural source to other people. [Wikipedia]

Colony (Society) Collapse Disorder.
Significant economic losses due to the disappearance of worker-bees living the young bees plenty of food and the queen. In the end the colony collapse. This can be natural or man-made or induced in which male worker bees are captured and put in transparent enclosures where they are observed for scientific purposes. The remaining colony is then left with capped brood abandoned something you will never see when male bees are present. Even though there is plenty of food the immature bees won't eat. They normally eat when adult male bees are present. They then die leaving the queen. In the end the colony collapse.

OVERVIEW

Following the theme in Volume I, everything no matter what
happens for a reason. Just like in the first volume, there is a
reasoning behind every event. I am going to highlight the
underlying principles behind the arguments in this Volume. My
assumptive hypothesis here is that there is a long-term War-
Contingency Plan. We have our goals, but we just don't know how
to achieve them. Everything that happens later, one way, or the
other is to help us shape our direction towards our goals.
Whatever happens, is also a way of how to achieve those goals
laid down in the contingency plan. The first of our goals is to
establish a law, a set of rules or any understanding that protects
us from any attacks and to establish an exclusion position simply
because this is the only way to avoid sabotage and savage attacks.
We need to protect ourselves. Self-defense.
There is a strong need to protect and strengthen our way of life as
a form of self-defense.
The exclusion stance which is based on grounds of sabotage and
savage attacks if included in power.
The idea here is to justify why things are the way they are. It has
nothing to do with any differences but simply because certain
groups lack the patriotic spirit and no matter what we do, their
aim is to carry out sabotage attacks. This was true during the
Geronimo era. Geronimo no matter what he would never change
his ways. His beliefs are different from ours and what we stand
for. All our efforts are to no avail. He will never appreciate our
system and our way of life. In that case, our aim is to take an
exclusion stance. Geronimo sees the American way of life as
manipulating and oppressive before they came, he had enjoyed
the land he believed was his forefathers. To him, he should not
bargain for what is his in the first place. The American system is to
deceive and manipulate his people how can he be part of a
system that is there to oppress his people. It's not that he doesn't
understand but the fact that he was robbed in the first place
is a cause of concern to him. He sees it as unfair that now they are

trying to include him in a system that first did damage to him which now to make things worse, is trying to manipulate him further. How can he be part of a system that first scared him? Until that is addressed, he can never be a part of that and addressing him would mean giving up the land back to him something that will mean the exodus of the Americans. Something that is considered as impossible as the new generations also claim to be part of this system. In that case, Geronimo will never be part of this because the initial wronging has not been corrected and such a justice system is flawed and cannot stand. He made it clear he cannot be part of this setting. In light of this, the Americans then realized that there is little they can do. They cannot give Geronimo back his land which he believed belonged to his forefathers and leave America. The Americans then incorporated those who want to be part of that system. Some of those were descendants of Geronimo. To safeguard themselves from Geronimo's further sabotage attacks they took an exclusion position and a way to achieve that exclusion position.

Fabrication of the level of threat posed by Geronimo.

An exclusion plan that fabricates the level of risk posed by Geronimo as a trigger of a vicious circle that will turn perceived risk into actual risk. Geronimo is viewed as uncivilized and all his life he has lived in the mountains preaching what is in the religious book of his forefathers. All he preaches is in the book written some 2000 years ago. He did quote a verse from this book and related it to modern-day settings. The USA had just invaded countries in the Persian Gulf and was viewed as looting the oil. He as the leader of his people and a messenger of his god has a duty to denounce such actions by the Americans. He quotes from a passage in the religious book that describes what will befall those looting his people's resources who are regarded as the infidels. Even if it was 400 years ago a rabbi or leader of the people like him would have said exactly the same thing. What he is saying is not something that comes from his head. He quotes a passage from his religious book. Then relates the passage to the present-day situation. Stating clearly, what that passage is referring to. Automatically since denouncing the looters, he becomes a terrorist. On the other hand, history has taught us also a lesson too. This fighting goes back to the beginning of time. Honestly, there is little we can do to solve the situation. We can't correct a wrong that happened centuries ago all we can do is include an exclusion clause. To be effective, we need to turn perceived risk into actual risk.

Perceived risk turns into real risk; a physiological mind game. Geronimo must preach every day to his people it's his duty in this life. Someone then goes around quoting Geronimo's sermons and then informs those responsible for security. In turn, everyone becomes alert. Perceived risk has turned to real and but nevertheless far-fetched. To include an exclusion clause to the whole situation the lies then resulted in actual persecution of Geronimo as he or his followers are questioned regarding the perceived risks he posed. Geronimo first might laugh off the whole thing.

"I live in a cave." he might argue.

"You have all the technology and money on how I can carry out such attacks from the mountains?"

Then people start getting ideas and somehow actual attacks are carried out. Now because what he preached has become real, we are therefore to exclude him, and this is our defense for the exclusion clause. Simply because he will never accept our way of life and for self-defense reasons, we can exclude him indirectly.

So, do you want to know why Geronimo can never be a leader or part of us? Simply because his mindset is to sabotage and destroy whatever we stand for. We can't correct the initially wrong nor can he accept anything to do with us.

How to enforce the exclusion: Colony Collapse Disorder studies. To understand Geronimo first we carry out an observational study to understand his way of life. We have a case study done 349 years ago this was a scientific study of some bees by a one Christopher Wren in 1654 who was an English astronomer, physicists, mathematicians, a scientist and an architecture born in

1632. We think this might apply here. Christopher Wren designed an octagonal three-floor man-made enclosure for bees. This was a transparent cage where bees can be held in captivity indefinitely without release and observed to understand their living habits. To evaluate the impact this will have economically to the remaining bees. The bees that were taken and put in these transparent cages were the worker-bees. If the worker-bees are removed, the bee's economy often suffers; fewer worker-bees means less production, fewer resources, and activities. If fewer resources mean fewer threats from bees as well. If leading worker-bees are removed, the colony will suffer, and that neutralizes the threat posed by a healthy functioning colony. In turn, Christopher Wren's other aim was to produce enough honey to replace expensive sugar with this English honey.

The putting of the male bees in the man-made enclosure would result in:

i] Presence of capped brood left.

When the worker-bees are available all the capped brood is looked after until it has hatched. Therefore, in a healthy colony, you won't find a capped brood that has been left. Usually, there is the inability of the left workforce to look after the brood.

ii] Presence only of the young male bees who are incapable of any attacks.

iii] Presence of a lot of food reserves as those left don't rob immediately. This is because the left bees will refuse to take and eat offered food as most need authorization or follow the adult worker-bees who obviously consume the food as they need the food for energy for carrying out their worker duties. The left young bees would only accept if the adult accepts as well and because the worker-bees are absent the young male bees will refuse the food. In turn, they will starve to death and the food brought to the queen-bee reduces, in turn, the colony shrinks, and the bees die of starvation and in the end the colony collapse.

iv] These experiments were carried out in order to turn England into Barbados during the 1650s according to one Benjamin Worsley, in Hartlib Papers, 28/2/2B [Ephemerides, 1651. The idea was to encourage locals to keep bees and harvest honey and replace expensive sugar with honey and wine with mead.

v] Christopher Wren's aim was to hold the bees in these cages indefinitely for scientific observations, studying how they live so that he can find a way to manipulate them using electromagnetic studies to enhance the production of honey in large quantities. The transparent man-made enclosure and its modern equivalent the Twin Towers and later the Guantanamo Bay transparent cages.

Christopher Wren's design was a three-story design. It had transparent glasses for observation with panels around it. An observer would watch the movement of honey bees inside. Wren's designed the man-made enclosure that was 12 inches deep and more than 18 inches across. It had three stories. Each story was separate from the other. There was though a continuous passage on the left side of the cage that runs from top to bottom linking all three stories together. This is the only passage that the bees used to get to the other zones. He noticed a strange behavior with the bees that no matter what, the bees never filled the top level with honey. Only the two stores. Somehow 317 years later we see the same ideas being applied to a building that is meant for humans. In the form of the World Trade Center Towers.

The Death Trap.

Okay, the idea might have sounded great 317 years ago applied to bees, not humans. I think the design did not take the risks of fires into consideration. The tower had 3 separate zones in each zone with floors. Indeed, whoever was behind the 9/11 attacks new of the drawbacks of the building and the position the planes impacted the towers were in such a way that the buildings would act as a death trap. I think someone else other than the terrorists had knowledge of this, and the idea was to create a death trap. The planes impacted at the exact critical points. The points where excess out of the buildings was through, the only way people could escape. The terrorists or someone with knowledge of Christopher Wren's plans and ideas and knowledge of the Twin towers was behind this. The idea was to create a situation where no one would escape. Everyone in the buildings was meant to die in there. This shows a devious and manipulating person planning to kill all those people in the building. It can't be just a terrorist attack. They knew if the planes hit where they did, no one would escape because the point the plane hit the North face inevitable blocked the express elevators. This meant that all the people on the top zone would die or be forced to jump something that happened on 9/11. Bear in mind what I said above; that Christopher Wren noticed that no matter what, the bees never made honey in the third top zone. The point the south tower was hit would result in the blocking of access to the express elevators that would take anyone faster out of the building. This was a death trap from the word go because even if there were lifts on each level these were local elevators for that zone. This also explained why people were being advised to wait in the towers instead of being told to run out of the building. The authorities knew the towers were death-traps. Where the planes impacted, was the lifeline for any hope of escaping. Just like the bees the people were trapped and just waiting to die. If it were bees, they could have jumped out and flew away. It is not surprising that people left with no option had to jump to their deaths; talking about the Falling man and others.

The World Trade Center Towers Destroyed: Aftermath.

After the destruction of the twin towers, the exclusion stance continued, and this time is enforced as people started being rounded up and a transparent enclosure just like the one designed by Christopher Wren for bees is now used to hold the suspects for the Society Collapse Disorder studies. The idea now becomes one of weakening the rest of the community to send fear and panic. The transparent enclosure made it look like everything was alright and acceptable as it was 'transparent' so that there was less resistance from the population. If the same people were put in a covered high-security enclosure a lot of people and rights groups would raise enough concern to order the release of these people. Anyone could see the captured 'guinea pigs' for the Society Collapse Disorder in transparent cages and could mistakenly assume that they are okay because they are in the open. Held indefinitely without any rights or chance to be released.

Tagging and serialization of human beings.

In order to monitor, study, command, incapacitate and exterminate the subjects involved in the future, a combination of drone and dog collar technology disguised as an implanted medical device [IMD] would be given to these captured and enclosed subjects after some time in captivity. Enclosed like that spending hours kneeling or sitting down will cause physical and physiological effects that will necessitate such IMDs.

Society Collapse.

The able-bodied men and potential leaders of tomorrow are rounded up and taken to Guantanamo Bay cages leaving the society without the future leaders of tomorrow. That has financial impacts on those left behind in society. The young become disgruntled, and that starts a vicious circle that more and more people will start feeling unfairly treated that in turn increases the risks and threats of attacks. In turn, the security is increased, and things tightened even harder and harder until the whole community is under surveillance and most of the young left after their fathers are taken into captivity to the transparent cages ends up being serialized and tagged. In the end, the state prevails as they use other means to squash down any resistance.

The Terrorism Assets Act.

Money is believed to fuel terrorism and the government are working relentlessly confiscating money from all suspected terrorist.

Reverse engineering as a means to an exclusion policy.

Unable to combat the attacks by the terrorists simply because they use unconventional methods and are hard to predict the state now must do what I am going to call here reverse engineering. To them, it's being proactive. They start looking at those with large amounts of money in their accounts and then target these. Now terrorists and wealth are linked. Anyone with wealth in their family becomes a "terrorist" and at risk. Anyone who deposits their wealth in banks abroad becomes a suspected terrorist or if it's a country then a nation funding terrorists. Society Collapse.

At last, the females left behind then start new families with provided males often of a different race or with higher social status to replace the caged ones who are destined to die in the cages without any hope of being freed. These males who are replacements of the caged man have a higher status than the caged man. The idea being that they will help the government's plan in that they would make everything look normal hiding the government's intent; that of enslaving through illegal tagging and serialization of the children of the men caged and their own as well without anyone raising suspicion. The children of all the men put in transparent cages at Guantanamo Bay will all be under state supervision. The new babies born to the women of the men at Guantanamo Bay all grow up under supervision and are tagged and serialized illegally simply because they have connections to people who have been at Guantanamo Bay caged indefinitely. In the end, the government achieves its goals of exclusion as fear, in the end, cause the society members to hide and run away as they grow, they are recycled through Guantanamo Bay. In the end, you have a second generation of children born to the new men while the men are free the children are subjected to surveillance forever and risk being tagged at birth. The vicious circle starts again until the society collapses and what remains are test subjects who can't fight or resist who are controlled remotely and are subjected to secret torture like dogs using an equivalent of dog collars only that the ones used are lethal. In the end, the state has achieved the Exclusion criteria at the same time has managed to protect its people and its way of life at the same time giving a good reason why Geronimo can never be inside White House as the President. Simply because he does not relate to the White House and everything it stands for.

Why War then?

First to reduce the nation's expenditure of oil and related

products that consume a lot of the nation's resources. War is the Superpower's task or way of correcting population growth and the easing of pressure on scarce resources. The world ecosystem must be balanced some have to die as long as we still have huge defense and military budgets.

Why the Colony or Society Collapse and its Guantanamo equivalent?

Population control as well. You will be shocked to find what your leaders are doing to control you from breeding like rabbits. Geronimo is like a pest you must use pesticides to control him no matter how harsh that sounds that is one of the reasons behind this. The Guantanamo Bay is a test pilot case that will pave way for forced secret abortions and family planning controls.

Terrorism as a horrific act.

There is no justification whatsoever for terrorists' acts because terrorists in most cases target civilians. Innocent people have nothing to do with what is going on politically or religiously. Obviously, the war is an unbalanced and surprisingly strong and more powerful nation is the one that often suffers casualties more than the terrorists themselves. The terrorists have developed an advanced system even though most are 'cavemen'. Some methods used are very advanced and have disastrous consequences even now some still baffles the most educated and intelligent members of the nation. That can only call for new strategies for combating terrorism. This could be the reason behind the Society Collapse studies and their implementation. Is there more to it than just the terrorists? Looking at the methods, stealthiest and precision often applied by these terrorists one can only conclude that the 'cavemen' has received a hand from some sophisticated foreign bodies or nations. The question is who? Very advanced knowledge of physics, astronomy, and mathematics is evident in the tools, planning, and execution of the terrorist activities. In Volume I, I have dealt with outsourcing as a means to an end. A way of realizing long term War-Contingency-Plans.

Building standards.

This should not be an issue with all the laws and regulations around, but care must be taken not to take things for granted and if in doubt there are a lot of qualified people who can test several methods and heights and capacities, etc. In some cases, the laws are there and regulations in place, but people can still break these especially where other factors play a role. In hard economic times, people tend to cut corners and more often the authorities might find it hard to enforce laws and regulations, but it is our responsibility to do whatever we can to make sure all buildings and infrastructure facilities are strong. What is the maximum height a building can be and how many lifts should be provided etc. are things to consider as well when building? Materials used like asbestos and lead should be monitored as well?

Moving with the times.

There are differences in development stages in which countries can be at a given time. Each country might be at a different level to the other and in some cases, some countries have well-documented events, laws, case studies, rules, and blueprints, etc. They might have developed an idea. A perfect idea to solve problems, but care must be taken into account. A thorough analysis of the political, economic and social environment at the time the experiment was made is important and should be analyzed in detail. This is true in the case of this man-made enclosure designed by this Christopher Wren for beekeeping. The idea was perfect at the time. Slavery had just been introduced in North America in 1654 the same year this Christopher Wren designed the transparent cage for bees. Now we see that some 317 years later the same methods have been applied not just to the Twin Towers but also to the Guantanamo Bay. We see the British scientific experiment done in 1654 now adopted and tested in real life by the Americans through the American equivalent of Christopher Wren, namely Larry Silverstein and the whole Bush Administration. That also raises suspicion if Hitler was also influenced by Christopher Wren's experiments of 1654, as the Auschwitz case is just like this Wren's experiment?

CHAPTER TWO

In Volume II things gets very interesting. Volume I covered the background information and Volume II goes deeper explaining the key players and factors and identifies the likely culprits manipulating the world to advance personal agendas at the expense of lives of innocent citizens. This volume will expose loopholes that are used by these culprits to evade justice. We know there is always a force behind such evil acts. We look at the ideas advanced in Volume I about the first beast, the second beast and their chief architect the dragon who with his fire-starting skills is doing whatever he can to turn everyone to the beast. To understand all this, I have pointed to the idea of mirror-image. This points to the ideas advanced in Volume I about the godfather-protégé paradigm. First, the reader must understand the underlying principles regarding the role of people in religious circles called the prophets. These people were regarded as holy as they needed to be holy as they were intermediaries between God and man. The prophet's role, therefore, was to bridge the unclean, unholy people to a holy omnipotent God. The prophet was between the two; holy and closer to God than everyone else and as a human is closer to mankind. His main job was to pass God's orders and instructions to the people. He was responsible for interpretations of events that he believed was from God. In his dreams or when he fell in a trance, God would pass the message for him to deliver to his people. He would see visions of events that were to happen in the future. Once he has had a vision, he would write it down on a scroll and seal the scroll and give it to the priests who would keep it. To prove that he was a true prophet he would tell the people his vision and interpret the vision before the actual event happens. When the event happens, then the people would know that he was a true messenger of God. This would be confirmed by the priest who would be holding the unopened scroll. In the temple after the event, the priest would read the scroll as a way of confirming the prophecy and acknowledging its fulfillment. That way the prophet gets credit as a true messenger of God that in turn whatever he said after that the people would listen to him. The people because of this and especially of the scrolls would have a sense of events to happen in the future. They had what you can call a guideline of how tomorrow's events would unfold. They had a sense of guidance about what tomorrow would be like. In other words, they could predict the future. God through his teaching would guide the people just like a parent would guide his or her son or daughter. It all depended in part on the people's actions too. It was not that easy to have the people destroyed. No. They were told that if you follow this path, it will lead you to such-and-such but if you follow this path, then you would experience this and that. Clearly, we see that it all depended on which course of action the people had taken. Choose the wrong path and surely this is what is in store for you. Disobey the advice then surely this action and this would happen to you. If you listen, then your future is guaranteed. Disobey and such-and-such would surely befall you. But what if it's like today when most people don't believe that there is a God? I bet even you the reader you might not believe that there is a God but still somehow the leaders of those days needed cooperation from their people to easily rule their people and make the people contribute to the economy through taxes. When it's God asking people to listen to him and to go to the temple to worship then most of the people would do that. If it was a man without any powers and authority most people would refuse. This is just human nature. Having said that, I want to draw the reader to a new way of thinking no matter your beliefs about God or the world. For those who do not believe in God with all respect of your beliefs, I want to ask you to be neutral as you read this report. Just like today, the more people learn and understand the world as a whole, the more they tend to view the world in a different way. The more you understand things the more likely you will discover operations of the world system. The more you become aware of certain things. You will know what is good and what is bad. You start questioning things. You start disbelieving people called prophets. Why? Simply because you now understand the world better. You now have realized that there is no God. In fact, the leaders at the beginning of civilization were having trouble collecting taxes from the people to fund their lavish lifestyle at the same time providing infrastructure and services. You know that in your circle the tradition has it that the events of the past have been narrated to the new generations through word of mouth. One of the scholars being told all these stories showed real enthusiasm that he listened to all the stories to such a point that he could tell them what happened and in what previous year even in his sleep. At the time the leader wanted to build and expand but was having difficulties convincing the people that he needed the little money they had in order to fund his lavish plans and goals. The people would not part away with the little they had. He realized that history had a tendency of repeating itself and that there were chances that certain events would reoccur given that action A or B has been chosen. He called that scholar with a sharp mind and asked him to sleep. He then invited the elders knowing that the scholar had an interest and a sharp memory. He then asks the scholar about things that happened in the past. Things and events, he had been told by the elders. Then cleverly he asked the scholar what would happen if say people did not listen to what he is saying and instead choose a different course of action. The scholar then would evaluate what occurred in the past when people followed a course of action. That in itself then acts like a predicition. If you don't listen and embark on certain activities, then surely you would experience these events A, B, etc. The scholar just because he can answer all their questions even in his sleep therefore there is a super being, a God. Man, only fear gods because these are believed to have created mankind and as such have more power and therefore should be feared. So, whatever is said and is from God is likely to be listened to. There is still a problem. The leader does not only want total obedience to easily run the country he also wants a way of collecting taxes that is linked to this God. He realizes that people would like to do good things and would give generously if taxes are associated with God. The leader then introduced offerings and sacrifices at the temple, money that ended up in the Emperor's coffers as taxes. We know when sacrificing means giving the little you have for a good cause. People would sacrifice and give generously as long as the giving is associated with good and God. We now see the rise of the idea that leaders or emperor at the time were leaders appointed by God in other words representatives of God. The leaders then associate themselves with the prophets who normally lived in the king's palace or were welcome to visit anytime. The prophets at that time became more powerful than the Emperors as they could choose and anoint who was to become a leader through the power of prediction. They could simply say don't vote for this king just because voting for this king would lead to all your destruction. Why? They might ask. Him as having abundant knowledge of past events and settings he might have envisaged that the-to-be Emperor or leader had links that can be manipulated to the destruction of the people simply because he had studied what happened in the past. The to-be Emperor felt robbed and manipulated that the prophet one they used to call a madman had more power than him. These prophets {scholars from the priest families taught from an early age] had to be dramatic to be believed to be holy and to have a special relationship with God. They had long hair and beard and acted strangely sleeping in the mountains where they would claim to have received a trance and a dream. The emperor then realized that something had to be done. He had to leverage the power balance. He asked the prophets to write down their dreams or predictions in advance so they can prove that he was telling the truth. The emperor at that time also passed a law of blasphemous which meant death by stoning for anyone who lies about having been sent by God deceiving people and taking the power from the emperor unnecessarily manipulating the people and turning them against the emperor. Most would be encouraged to refuse to pay taxes. This is because the prophets denounced the lavish lifestyles of the Emperors. In the end, the prophets soon became the enemies of the Emperor and were killed, and we have Jesus suffering the same fate. The main problem was that these emperors were associated with evil acts, yet they preached that they were sent by God, yet the people knew that God was holy and good. In the end, the people listened to the prophets more than to the Emperor whom they saw as robbers of the little money they had. The Emperors had weakened the prophets by asking them to write everything down. He could easily open the scrolls and read them. We also know that these Emperors were forbidden to enter the house of the priest to preserve the scrolls so that the Emperors won't read these. So how would the Emperor declare they are representatives of God when they are doing evil acts? That raises the idea of Beasts on earth. The people at the time had realized that there might not even be a God. The emperor wanted a way of collecting money where he would ask everyone to offer sacrifices and offerings at the temple. To carry on with both evil and good acts the Emperor then commands the prophet to write the account of the beasts that is believable to the people. God after giving mankind the power to think for himself found mankind very knowledgeable to question his authority. Of these people, some had evolved to God's status. Here developed the idea of the beasts. To be believable since people now knew that there might not be a God. The prophet probably persuaded by the Emperor who still wanted to be feared and to do both good and evil and still be regarded as sent by God declared that man has evolved to the status of God. And such men were on earth. Something that gives them an immediate presence and something that can be believed. These humans are like the beast with all the features of animals and power too. God briefly has given them powers to imitate him. He has delegated his duties to these humans as they have become like God himself and for a period are given powers by God to do what God does that is to maintain the world balance. Killing some people just like what God does through nature. That could defend the evil acts of the Emperors and be still viewed as appointed by God. Whenever an Emperor commits evil acts, it's simply in the name of God, just like God would send an earthquake to kill maybe a thousand people to free up space. These emperors would do the same but since they have no powers to command nature, they must devise ways of killing the people to do the same as God. Just like in Revelations 13v 1-18 these emperors are viewed by God through the prophet as beasts. God is holy and as such cannot be associated with such evil and savage animals. But he admitted that these beasts have eaten the forbidden fruits and they are now more knowledgeable to an extent that they themselves have equaled God's status and as such can now live forever but on one condition; that they must kill continually.

Genesis 3v22

22 Then the LORD God said, "Behold, the man has become like one of us, knowing good and evil. And now, lest he reaches out his hand and take also from the tree of life, and eat, and live forever. Since the beasts have become like God and they can live forever and as such would need to act like God too killing people to alleviate the pressure, such was God's fear out of love for mankind that that kind of life is unbearable to humans with feelings and flesh. Gods have spirits and are spirits. The pain of killing would only drive mankind to kill more and more it's like once you start you can stop. Such a person cannot have been sent and have been appointed by God, but such a beast has gained such status through forbidden means, nevertheless. As such just to prove a point God is going to delegate his duties to that person so that he self-destructs due to the pain associated with his task of killing to balance nature. This beast realized it was a tough challenge as it developed a lethal head wound. Another beast arose from the earth to serve the first beast. This beast has healing powers and is given powers by the first beast and these two beasts now work hand in hand with the second beast

appointed by the first beast summoning people and encouraging them to listen and worship the second beast. This second beast to make everyone obedient it must trick, deceive and manipulate everyone no matter what status they have. The rich, poor, old and young alike. Somehow this beast must tag or give serial numbers to everyone giving them marks so that they are easily identified. This is like a pass or license to identify each person and those with these marks would be allowed to sell and buy. This beast's duty is to enroll people into the cult of the first beast giving instructions to kill. I have explained above that fear for God was automatic and it was easy for the people to obey instructions associated with God. The people have become very clever, clever to note that God can't be good and evil at the same time. They are now clever to say no to the emperor who used God's image to manipulate the people. Now the emperors have come up with a second plan.

"Ok it is not God behind all this." the Beast might say.

"It is me the beast. I now believe that God is jealous of mankind and he would want us to stay in the dark so that we rely on him all the time with stupid handouts when we can be as God and rich and powerful as him. I say to hell with that, in fact, he is aware I can do a better job than him, so all you fox know that everything is under control. I have the license signed by God himself to kill. Every act needs not questioning because it is indirectly authorized and approved by none other than God himself." the Beast could brag.

The beast realized that he has no God's powers to cause natural disasters and that he needed someone. In the stories told by the prophets, the emperor then realized that the most feared calamity was death by fire and Sulfur. Now we have a dragon who breathes fire as their baker who sets fire everywhere to turn people to these beasts. We now have a complete triangle. The first Beast, the second Beast, and the dragon. They all work together to achieve one goal.

We know now that just like today those who did not believe that there was a God and that the bible was written to manipulate mankind into obedience still had another convincing theory that of the Beasts. Okay, there is no God but there are beasts too clever and too powerful to do the acts which if there was a God this God would be doing the same. This hypothesis is more convincing. The Beast is here on earth. He can be seen. He is like a man, yet he has God's powers. All his killings and acts need not questioning. These emperors collected and ordered events of the past to be written down and used to manipulate the people and to a major extent to be used as prediction tools of the future. They would simply look at what happened in the past and predict the future. The Emperors during their time had noted also that history had a tendency of repeating itself as man 2000 years ago lived the same way as today's man. Only that the threats and conditions have changed but life is still the same. Some people still maintain the culture and ways of doing things like many centuries ago. They opened the old scrolls and learned what happened in the past and tried to use that knowledge to solve today's problems and in some situations recreating the events stage by stage just like in the past designed to achieve the same results. This makes them the same as Film Directors. They have a script they know every move and how the situation will unfold. They make self-fulfilling prophecies. They claim to know the future and how things will unfold. For a small fee or a favor, they gather a large following and appoint whoever listens to them. Just like the trickery scholars who studied past events memorizing everything then claim to have seen visions sent by God becoming prophets and part of a huge web of deceit run by Emperors in order to easily command the people and collect taxes. Don't forget the bible urges the people to give Caesar what belongs to Caesar. Something that can be regarded as a trickery way of maximizing the collection of taxes. We have seen very prominent people in recent years who are believed to have foretold events that ended up happening. These people have been believed to have prophesied about world events that ended up happening. They are credited for having foresight about future events. Some just because of that are regarded as great predictors of the future.

But are they? Or they are just part of a cult. Yes, a cult where membership is defined by the presence of a mark on the forehead or on the hand or some serial number or tagging. Such marks and identification make one belong to this cult. The leader of this cult is the second beast whom we know is answerable to the first beast. Membership of this cult guarantees one to participate in the buying and selling. But buying and selling of what? We know this makes sense if this is in the buying and selling of shares or stock trading. Wait a minute this makes sense. Membership to a cult that deals in shares everyone with a mark on hand or forehead or if identified somehow can guarantee those people insight information in share dealing that will benefit them and make them rich. This is a cult that depends on the members for information through self-fulfilling prophecy to control world events.

The Trickery.

We know people claimed to have foreseen the future and predicted what was going to happen. Were these really prophecies or clever tricks by the second beast through dreams just like with scholars or prophets in the past? That explains why I am arguing that the second Beast is behind all these events. We know from Revelations 13v11-17 that it is written that the second Beast manipulates the people using tricks to turn people to worship the first beast. Those who refuse would be killed as ordered by the second Beast. All those who prophesy about future events are they really prophets? Or just members recruited by the second Beast. We know technological advancement just like in hypnosis is used to command people in dreams something I will look at in later chapters. People can be given instructions in dreams to carry out activities deemed necessary for the cult to achieve its desired objectives. A lot has changed since the days of the prophet, but the message and activities are still the same. The second Beast knows its role in all this and as such are doing everything to make the prophecy in the bible come true. Therefore, for the clever few a bible is a trendsetter in terms of advanced technological achievements. Every human being who has reached a certain level of understanding. A man who has achieved the status of God will understand the need to read and understand the bible. The bible is a manual of how to carry out activities mainly designed to conquer the world and rule the rule. It preaches peace to those whose land is colonized and occupied. It encourages not to fight if invaded. It speaks of prophecies of a future world led by a God-appointed leader to unite all mankind. It seems it was written by the colonialist. Nevertheless, what matters to us is the fact that it is used even now to guide world events. People with knowledge of the bible are using the bible to solve today's problems. What are regarded as predictions are not predictions as such but pre-planned and carefully directed acts to achieve a goal? 9/11 attacks are no different. People have simply assessed the current problems and went to look for answers in the bible and throughout past events to solve current problems. Simply because the bible has all the events for the past 2000 years. That points to the 9/11 attacks as pre-planned and directed as in film making by the second Beast from the word go. This is not supernatural but simply manipulating the skills and cleverness of scholars who read past events, assessed the situation and used these case studies to solve the current problems. Having said that, you can now see why I dwelt much on the art of prediction and its roots in the bible with the prophets. Through want we know as hypnosis the Emperors were able to question the scholars about events in the past and which course of action to take while they were in trances. These made the scholars more feared and important that most had more power than the emperors. They anointed who was to be Emperor and or king.

The art of forecasting and prediction rather than a prophecy.

So how can the second Beast solve today's problems and turn people to the first Beasts?

I] They need to account for everyone rich or poor, young or older, king or slave. That gave rise to the need to give serial numbers to everyone in the disguise of medical records the so-called personal computer chips. Again, the bible directs technological advancement and used to solve current problems. To control the people all these people should belong to a cult. A mark should be given to each one of them on the right hand or forehead to identify them and as proof of belonging to a group. The second Beast will take records of each one may be through tagging at birth. Collecting and knowing the information about everyone requires a lot of money. Bearing this in mind the cult should be involved in a form of fundraising or investment. All it's people those in the cult with a mark or a serial number will be able to buy and sell that participates in share dealings. This is in the bible written more than 2000 years ago even before we had stock markets but something happening today. That can answer some people who say that it's stupid to believe in the bible, but it doesn't hurt to read it. The common belief among those who have eaten the forbidden fruit, whom God regarded as like him is that every prophecy must be fulfilled. People turn to the bible for ideas about technological advancement. From Revelations 13 comes the tagging system, medical devices to record and identify everyone from birth throughout. We have ideas about satellite to track and monitor cult members. We have a share of dealing with technological ideas. We have power structures with one person who can take the place of God on earth. Okay going back to the point at hand is this prophecy or clever forecasting and prediction. The cult needs to raise loads of money to collect information about everyone. That requires huge sums of money. That requires sophisticated ways of deceiving people which is the second Beasts' task as in Revelation 13v 11-17. The beast must know every event that happened in the past and use that information to raise money. This is the main point behind all this. So, in short for every event in the world if we are going with this line of thinking there is a monetary value to each. In most cases, the event happens to deceive the people, in other words, to make people blind about the money reasons for every event. Money is, therefore, the sole reason for any events associated with the second Beast for the second Beats will require a load of gadgets and software to collect a lot of information and develop a technology that will deceive the people. Don't forget also I said that the beasts must act like God killing people too, therefore, the main reason behind all the 9/11 attacks and other terrorists' attacks is the need to go to war to kill as many as they can get the oil resources cheaper son as to save money, they would otherwise spend on oil products. Money they will use to make Weapons of Mass Destruction [WMDs] and set a time-bomb to destroy more than half of the world's population. The Beast will need some form of technology to talk to the people in their dreams just like in the old days with the prophets talking to God in dreams and trances. In Genesis 3v22 God acknowledged that some humans have attained that status as his. They have a vast knowledge of the world. Their eyes have been opened and they see things like God. These people have God's approval and for two years God will give them his go-ahead. So, if the second Beast is approved to act like God then he must act like God or at least act like what to be expected of a God. God, we know speaks in dreams to his prophets. The second Beast will need money as well to develop gadgets that will enable it to talk to its prophets in dreams. We know that this is derived from the art of hypnosis having that in mind we can surely say that technology exists today. This will be very important when I look at the real culprits behind the 9/11 attacks and all world events. God gives dreams called visions to his prophets of events to come and these events must come true for the prophet to be regarded as credible and one sent by God. The Beast who is temporarily assigned to do God's work will have to be able to give visions to his followers too. The technology and gadgets are in existence today. The Beast is working clockwise nonstop to gather information and money resources to achieve all predictions in the bible. To be able to communicate and interpret and collect information the second Beast shall be everywhere to collect and send a message. This brings me to the role of the film director. God in the bible is the mighty film-director coordinating every effort running around taking the film and coordinating every move. That explains why God must be a spirit in order to be everywhere coordinating every event just like a film director. He has powers to command nature to carry out activities. The second

Beast must match God as the film director being everywhere to coordinate every scene of the movie. As such he will need sophisticated satellite and GPS tracking and recording system to receive the message and translate these and send these. Now it seems the software to do this remotely without the physical presence is absent that could explain why you see the second Beast all the time. Just like in Revelations the second Beast must manipulate and deceive people pretending that he has software to make people communicate to each other in a sixth sense-like setting but in fact, all these people are being controlled by software based on viral mutations a weapon used on them without their knowledge a Weapon of Mass Destruction. A crime under international law.

Advanced knowledge of the event.

The second Beast manipulates people and offers to help people cross the river just like the prophet Moses in the bible. The second Beast has vast records of past events in scrolls, paper and soon on digital gadgets stored in space. The second Beast relies on past events to predict the future. It assesses likely scenarios of outcomes to deduced from a given case study. Following that then proposes a solution that will solve the problem of the person in question at the same time leaving doors open to the money for the person in question and itself. Like I said every reason has a monetary value to it.

9/11 attacks and advanced knowledge of the second Beast.

The second Beast assessed the situation before 9/11 and realized that a solution was needed and as such went back in time and looked for a solution. After finding a similar solution then using this case study, then he wrote a film script and using this film script to coordinate the 9/11 attacks for a healthy $2,3 trillion share. This does not end there. 9/11 was used as a prediction to guide its members on the courses of action to take to make a lot of money in share dealing or buying cheap and selling dear.

9/11 as a Film Script based on the Great Fire of London 1666.

The second Beast has seen that the problems before 9/11 were similar although not identical to the situation in London 1666. The

main theme is the same. Fire can send a clear message at the same time $2,3 trillion was a lot of money. He compared the people involved in the Great Fire of London and come up with a script and cast based on players in the 1666 fire of London.
9/11 attacks The Death Trap: Film Script (fictional title) The recreating of the Great London fire as the 9/11 attacks Film Script based on 1666 Great Fire of London.
The Actors.
Christopher Wren played by Larry Silverstein.
Christopher Wren was a great mathematician whose work was known by the great Isaac Newton, a scientist, and a great architect. Born 1632 he helped found the Royal Society after being a professor of astronomy. For more than four years he taught astronomy that involved teachings on space travel. As a mathematician, he knew physics as well. He was well vested in physics and engineering and because of these two subjects he developed a lot of interest in architecture. In the designing of buildings. Years before the great fire he had been commissioned to design buildings. In 1664 and 1665 he had designed buildings, a theater, and a chapel. Interested even more in architecture he traveled to Paris where he observed the French's building style and on his return to London it can be assumed that he relished an opportunity of putting London in the right direction. He knew London according to a one Samuel Pepys was poorly designed with narrow streets and overcrowding. The Great fire of 1666 was like a break-through for Wren. He had been given an opportunity to put his great ideas on a blueprint and design the city of London. We see an ambitious young man only 31 years at the time of the fire having been to France and seen great buildings in Paris having liked the French baroque probably wanted to adopt the same for buildings in London. I can only assume that he had plans even before the fire of redesigning the city of London. He had assumed that such a grand plan would be received by everyone involved with great appreciation but to his surprise, after the fire, his plans were rejected. One of the reasons was that the king, King Charles II did not see the need for new plans as there was nothing wrong

with the plans. The building practice at that time was the problem. Secondly, the landowners refused to give up the land preferring to keep their properties. After designing more than fifty churches he was given the task of being the Royal surveyor looking after all government buildings getting knighted in the process. By 1675 he was asked to design the Royal Observatory at Greenwich. This was through a request he received, a commission by the King. His dedication and interest made him the King's favorite in custody of all government buildings but of interest here was the Royal Observatory at Greenwich. The idea advanced in Volume I is that these buildings were not just buildings but specially designed and build buildings to serve a special purpose. He left a legacy and at that time when he died people could still see him just by looking at the surrounding buildings most of which he had designed himself. His most notable presence was through his efforts and hard work of building more than fifty churches in London. Religion was associated with the monarchy, with kings and power as well. That gave him a standing among the people to be bestowed a knighthood years later. Of interest to the report is his involvement in founding the Royal Society and in the designing and building of the Royal Observatory building at Greenwich.
Royal Observatory Greenwich.
This played a great role in astronomy and navigation. This was built in 1675 by Wren and supported by Robert Hooke built largely out of recycled material. This was the first built scientific research facility in Britain. A one John Pond installed a time-ball at the Royal Observatory that dropped every day at 1 pm. This time the ball was dropped manually until the year 1852 when it was dropped automatically with an electrical signal from a place called the Shepherd Master Clock. In 1894 a French terrorist tried to bomb the building but failed as a bomb exploded before he reached the building.
The Oliver Cromwell Period.
In 1658 he was a professor of astronomy at Gresham College Oliver Cromwell died and the college was occupied by the military. A lot of gunpowder was left in the houses and schools of

London. This had been brought into the city during the Oliver Cromwell wars.

The breakthrough.

On 27 August 1666, he submitted a plan of the dome of St Paul's Cathedral which was accepted in principle in Oxford. One-week later London was in flames. This gave Wren a great opportunity he had probably been waiting for. He headed to London at the news with much enthusiasm. While London was still in flames between 5 to 11 of September, he submitted plans to the king of a new London. Having been to France he incorporated French building styles Gardens of Versailles into the plans and Roman building styles in his plans for a new London. There was competition from others though. On 13 September Charles II gave his desire to adopt a new plan. Wren just like the king and others had assumed that it was going to be easy to reconstruct again. They had assumed that the people who owned the land would be easy to move and compensate. This turned out to be difficult. The compensation bill was too great, and most people had refused to be located. The land survey cost was great. The result was the rebuilding Act of 1667.

The Building Act of 1667.

The need to rebuild led to the rebuilding Act in which all buildings were made of brick and stone only. The Act also defined the maximum number any building could go high. After his plans were disapproved as unfeasible Wren was instead appointed as one of the Commissioners to oversee the construction of the building making sure that correct materials were used, and the streets were wide enough. After 1667 a Fire Court heard settlement claims brought by the owners of destroyed houses.

Larry Silverstein who plays Christopher Wren and looks like him [see images on Google] him too is a businessman involved in property and real estate development. As an enthusiastic developer, Silverstein won the bid to build World Trade Center 7 and showed interest in acquiring all the World Trade Center Buildings. Port Authority of New York gave him a lease for the WTCs. He signed a deal on July 24, 2001. He got insurance that covered the buildings each for $3,55 billion. After the attacks, he failed to collect the insurance money. The insurance citing that the attacks were one event meaning they can pay around $3,55 billion. He argued that the events were two separate ones, so each building was to be given a separate payout meaning a total of $7 billion. In the end, he was only awarded $4.55 billion. Silverstein retained rights to build 150, 175, and 200 Greenwich Street offices. Note that Wren had built the Royal Observatory in Greenwich now we see Silverstein building towers in Greenwich street in the USA Newyork whereas Wren built in London England. Bear in mind that Newyork and London are Mirror-Image sister cities the idea advanced in Volume I. Just like Wren soon after the attacks Silverstein showed an interest in the rebuilding of the buildings. He managed to rebuild 7 World Trade Center with One World Trade Center being designed and built by someone else. Minoru Yamasaki.

Designed the original World Trade Center Building. He is well known for his aluminum building called the Reynolds Metals Company Building. Aluminum served as the main component of World War II aircraft and ship infrastructure but after the war new uses were drafted including its use in buildings. Reynolds metals re-cast aluminum salvaged from warships and planes and recycled it here for domestic use. After the war and during the 1950s Reynolds campaigned for the commissioning of aluminum in modern architecture. Reynolds hired Yamasaki for what they called the dramatization of aluminum into architecture. Yamasaki built the World Trade Center incorporating the Gothic architecture mainly used for churches and cathedrals. The main features involve the use of rib vaults and flying buttresses.

King Charles II played by George W Bush.

England was going through a rough time as three events nearly brought it on its knees. These were the Anglo-Dutch wars of 1665-1667. This was a war fought to control trade routes. England had no money paying the Royal Navy personnel with debt vouchers they had just been out of the first Anglo-Dutch war in which they won. The Dutch were prepared for the second Anglo-Dutch war as they had bought new ships. The British have no money to buy or build new ships. The war was fought for the control of lucrative trade routes and the control of the seas. The British after the first Dutch wars were engaged in the Anglo-Spanish wars of 1654-1660. These wars were fought as commercial rivalry increased. This weakened Britain financially. Charles II requested farmers to join the war leaving women on farms and that resulted in a famine that might have caused food shortages with the resultant plague of 1665. This devastated London with as much as 7000 deaths per week in September 1665. That led the king too fled to Salisbury leaving the people alone. When winter arrived the plague, then receded making the king return to London. The plague was believed to be caused by rats. February 1666 the King had returned to London. The following season was characterized by hot and dry weather. This weather saw the start of the Great Fire of London. The fire is believed to have been started somewhere in Pudding lane at a bakery of a one Thomas Farriner who had a contract with the King to supply biscuits for the Royal Navy ships. Unlike during the great plague, the King stayed in London and fought the fire helping to create firebreaks. He and his brother tackled the fires of London that burned for days relentlessly destroying 13,200 houses, 87 churches, the cathedral, the Royal exchange and two-thirds of the city living 70 000 of the 85 000 inhabitants homeless. We know from the account of a one Samuel Pepys that the king played a major role in the tackling of the great fire. Taking over from the hesitant Mayor Thomas Bloodworth. He ordered the destruction of the houses to create firebreaks as the fires raged. This was the common firefighting method at the time. Samuel's account places the King and his brother at the heart of the firefighting team. This gave him back his respect among the people and showed his commitment to his people patching back his reputation among the people. After the fire even though, new plans were drawn and submitted to be considered as the new plans of London the king for the unforeseeable reason stuck to the original plans. Compensation claims from land and property owners at the time were very high and the cost of the surveyors were huge too. Some people who owned land refused to change ownership making most of the plans unfeasible.

King Charles II is played by George W Bush.

In the script, I named the Death Trap. After being the Governor of Texas, Bush was elected President of America. Initially, he had ambitious domestic policies but all that changed due to the 9/11 attacks. Bush had a narrow victory over Al Gore. The closeness of the results meant a recount of the Florida votes. There were accusations of vote tampering and suppression. Since getting into office his ratings were around fifty percent and after 11 September there were spikes with his best approval rate reaching as high as 92% the best for any USA President. The 9/11 attacks saw his approval ratings shoot-up from nearly 53% to 85% within the first two years then declined when the war started. There was a spike from 50% when he entered office to 85% when the 9/11 attacks occurred. Another spike was soon after 1 February 2003 when the Columbia disaster occurred. Spikes in approval are associated with incidents of the 9/11 attacks and the space shuttle disaster and his role during a time of need. On 10 September Donald Rumsfeld announced that the President's office at the Pentagon had misplaced a staggering $2,3 trillion. That could have meant low approval rates just before the attacks. In short, I think it's open to anyone to suggest that just like the king Charles II his approval rates before the incidence were low. They all had empty coffers. The missing $trillions could have sent a bad picture showing Bush as a president, not in charge of his own administration. Even though some criticize him for acting very slow the day of the attacks, he took a strong stance that made him gain back the people's backing. He dealt with the situation as the Americans expected. It should be noted also that in most cases there is a two-year period window between the time of a shocking event to time its impact will still be felt by the people. That could explain his approval ratings dropping in January 2003. A second shocking event the Columbia disaster then caused the spiking of the approval rating graph. His ratings also increased during the invasion of Iraq but slowly declined as anti-war protests increased throughout.

Mayor Thomas Bloodworth played by Rudy Giuliani the Mayor of Newyork.

When the fire started on 2nd September 1666 the mayor Thomas Bloodworth was woken up by the people but played the fears down suggesting that a woman could piss the fire out. He then went back to bed. Little had he known that the climatic conditions of dry weather, heavy easterly winds, and the high hot temperatures were ideal for the fire to quickly destroy the houses. The fire destroyed as much as 300 houses by the next day. The mayor as such was supposed to quickly get permission from the owners of the houses and order the breaking down of these houses to create a fire break. He was also obliged to meet the King and get further permission instead it seemed he had disappeared the next day leaving a one Samuel Pepys approaching the king. The king soon after ordered the destruction of the houses in the path of the fire. The houses were destroyed with hooked poles. The mayor was nowhere to be seen leaving the King in the bucket line passing the buckets to fight the fire. Samuel Pepys's account suggested that a lot of material like gunpowder left after the Oliver Cromwell wars intensified the fire. Some accounts suggested that gunpowder was used to create fire breaks. The sound of explosions made the people suggest that the French were invading. We don't hear about the mayor until after the fire. Giuliani was the mayor of Newyork. During the attacks even though he was near the World Trade Center he ordered a stand-down when World Trade Center 7 began to burn. He did not order the tackling of the fires in building seven. After the terrorist attacks of 1983, he had asked the Emergency and disaster office to be located in WTC7 something that was criticized by others. Just like in 1666 there were laws in place, but the builders were not following these laws using forbidden materials.

The mayor of London Bloodworth was not a happy man the previous year having had to be involved in the movement of corpses during the plague. He had seen the effect and impact of the plague. His job was to run the city, but it seemed that he had become like the undertaker, running the city of London ordered the removal of corpses for burial in carts. The people had no money even if he had enforced the laws there was little the people could have done. It can be inferred that probably when the fire happened this was a relief. At last the only solution; he might have said. That could also explain why he did not order the destruction of the houses to create fire breaks. Fire was the only solution. Although some might have argued that he needed permission from the owners to order the breaking of the houses nevertheless he might have wished for this fire. This is true considering Pepys remarks that he seemed unconcerned if the fire was going to spread. Pepys went further to write that he reckoned that Bloodworth was stupid and a weak man in his eyes. This was due to his hesitation to order the destruction of the houses to contain the fire but if you know what had happened just a few months before that then he might have arrived at a different conclusion. The plague had claimed nearly a hundred thousand people in London alone in a year or more. To the mayor, the fire was a solution. To kill all the rats and it seemed also that the great fire caused the plague to recede. The World trade center buildings were now old, and some offices were unoccupied. Even though there were building laws guiding builders and construction companies. It seemed that these laws were not followed. We know the stairways of the World Trade Center were very narrow as compared to the number of people in the buildings with the resultant that these were clogged during the escape. This is reminiscent of the narrow streets of London which were crowded making it hard for people to escape the fire. London was built of wood and thatch materials as well as the lead instead of the recommended bricks and steel. The designer of the World Trade Center was Minoru Yamasaki. Yamasaki had a few months back before designing the WTC had designed an aluminum building for the Reynolds Metals Company. The Reynolds were trying to attract new customers and advocate for the adoption of aluminum in architecture and building development. We know the reason why the Port Authority of Newyork leased the towers was because they had passed their 'sell-by date'. They were old and energy inefficiency as compared to other new buildings. Even worse, they had plastic-covered asbestos. The time they were built asbestos was not a major issue. New standards have meant the removal of these asbestos floors. Removing all the asbestos could have cost the Port Authority as much as a billion when they were worth less than that. Larry Silverstein lease the towers with the hope of rebuilding them.

CHAPTER THREE

Samuel Pepys played by Donald Rumsfeld.

He was in the Royal Navy. He wrote the account of what happened during the great fire of London. At times he took the role of the Mayor going to the king to report the fire incident. He stayed around London writing everything that happened in his account. Donald Rumsfeld as the secretary of state and defense was a military man at the time of the 9/11 attacks. He took account of the balance sheet and noticed that a whopping $2,3 trillion was missing from the pentagon. Concerned and something he saw as his duty and responsibility approached the nation and informed everyone on national television that the money was unaccounted for and missing.

Colony Collapse Disorder: Man-made enclosure for scientific observation May 1654.

Christopher Wren's major field of study was mathematics, engineering, astronomy, physics, and architecture.

Christopher Wren while at the All Souls College in Oxford England constructed a transparent man-made enclosure for housing insects that were used for experimenting and scientific research. The main idea was to scientifically research what would happen is worker male bees were removed from a swarm of bees leaving the queen bee, a lot of food and the other bees involved in caring duties with very small immature bees. As the worker bees are enclosed, there are economic losses as the able-bodied are no longer available to work. There were widespread economic losses and lack of the pollinating honey bees all caused crops to fail. The reduction of worker bees caused population reduction as well. A population control tool. Christopher Wren proposed a three-story transparent beehive. The bees were able to move within all the divisions. An observer could see inside from outside through the glass panels. The observer could easily see the honey flowing down. The only downfall of Wren's designed was that he was not able to foresee the fact that bees worked downward. Nevertheless, his design offered a chance of increasing the number and variety of bees within one containment. The idea that the enclosure was transparent made it easily accepted it removed the fear and moral correctness associated with keeping bees in enclosures. People are easily likely to accept open transparent enclosures than covered enclosures. Less rejection and opposition even if it is wrong to remove bees from natural habitats to man-made enclosures. The idea behind these enclosures was to study the ways of the bees so as to design ways of controlling those bees according to a one Sir Cheney Culpeper. The man-made enclosure promoted by Samuel Hartlib, who was a neighbor of the above Samuel Pepys during the great fire was meant to study the bees and then replace sugar with the English Honey and wine with mead. Hartlib just like Wren hoped to present his findings to the Commonwealth Trade and Foreign affairs so that the method can be given official approval or patronage. Hartlib acknowledged that his model just like Wren was to provide a pious or vain industry and good husbandry as inbreeding of an animal.

Samuel Hartlib and the Council of trade's goals were to 'turn England into Barbados'. The idea was to create plenty of honey and substitute expensive white sugar, used in food and brewing. Guantanamo Bay detention camp established in 2002. [Similar to Auschwitz camp all of which I think were based on the work of this Christopher Wren]

This is based on Christopher Wren's transparent man-made enclosures for keeping bees as I have pointed out above for scientific purposes and to find a way to replace sugar with English honey; that is Weapons of Mass Destruction in the form of Implanted Medical Devices. The idea is to study the captured

males, the resulting economic hardship among left families with the idea to substitute these with 'English honey'. Often accused of breeding like animals just like Christopher Wren and the man who perfected his designs, Hartlib. The idea just like in 1654 was to provide a vain or pious industry or a way of keeping people as animals indefinitely. They used Christopher Wren's design as well of making everything transparent. The idea of concentration camps and enslaving is easily acceptable even though it's wrong. The fence gives people the idea that the detainees were not ill-treated yet it's a real fundamental breach of human rights. Here we have that idea again of godfather-protégé. The Americans being taught how to abuse and get away with murder by none other than the British. Mind you this was in the 1650s, way back that most people of today can't be asked to research what happened then. It's like a manual. That also supported the idea of the Mirror-Image. Whether it is good or not, I will let you the reader decide. This will be advanced later in the report when I link this to the financial status of the people accused and or killed regarding all this. Most of these people being detained and killed are heirs to vast fortunes left by their fathers. Take Osama Bin laden for example. It is a fact that his father left a $7 billion fortune. Given that America was missing $2,3 trillion a day before the 9/11 attacks is it not also a good reason to try to cut the heir from inheriting all this money? Let's just say for arguments' sake the $2,3 trillion missing from pentagon was not missing in the sense of disappearing from the pentagon but because they spent this money on oil purchases and related products. Let us also recall what the former USA president said; Eisenhower, that "nationalizing the canal was not the same as nationalizing oil wells [which] exhaust the nations [financial resources]."
In light of that, we can see that the USA is experiencing may be increased costs due to the high fuel or oil bill. That could be because of the wars with warplanes needing jet fuel. Another common point, especially in Britain, is the fact that any money that has once been accounted for in their books somehow has to be recovered and not allowed to leave the country. If they have

purchased something say oil. They get the oil still they will pursue after the money until they have recovered that money back even if it means killing that person.

Gamal Abdel Nasser stunt.

One more important factor here is the fact that George W Bush might have done the Gamal Nasser stance. We know that Nasser used a clever tactic in order to take back the Suez Canal from the British and the French. When he was addressing a rally in 1956, he mentioned the Frenchman's name thirteen times as giving orders to the military to confiscate the Suez Canal from the westerners. George W Bush might have actual copied Nasser and when he said "our freedoms were attacked" he was giving orders to do that. Infringing people's human rights and violating privacy laws.

Cause for Concern.

The main cause of concern here is the fact that America is adopting directly or indirectly methods developed by the British in the 1600s that is 400 years ago and applying all these in recent years or it's not taking its position in the world by kissing British's ass. The British have seen all this they might tell America that we have seen it we have done it there is nothing you can tell us. It's shocking that something done by the British in 1654 is applied to the USA as recent as 2002 and Guantanamo Bay is still open. Ideas developed or advanced by Christopher Wren in 1654 when the British were as corrupt as never before with no acknowledgment of human rights at all. Where I can only infer that racism was at its highest. The year 1654, this Christopher Wren constructed the man-made enclosure equivalent to Guantanamo Bay was the year North America first experienced slavery even though slavery was there for more than 150 years worldwide.

First Slavery 1654 North America.

Slavery first introduced in North America in 1654 by a one Anthony Johnson an Angolan black man once indentured but a free man at the time. He went to court and declared that he was entitled to the lifetime services of one John Cazara, a black man. This was the first-time slavery was acknowledged by the courts. John Cazara argued that he was an indentured servant and that

Johnson had forced him to work past his term. He was freed and went to work for a one Robert Parker. Then Johnson sued Parker, and the court declared that John was a slave and acknowledged the rights of free blacks to own slaves. In 1654 on the other side Barbados was England's favorite colony based on slavery and sugar plantation.

Christopher Wren's Obsession with the moon that leads to the invention of telescopes and micrometers.
Obsession with the moon meant Wren spending time observing it ended up designing an artificial one that he showed the King. He did not stop there; he went on to inject substances into the dog's bloodstream as an experiment. He did studies to improve the microscope and telescope too and, in the end, improving these. Wren designed a lunar ball and handed this to the king. This was through his obsession with the moon.
Cycloid discovery.
'In other words, this is a curve generated by a curve rolling on another curve.' [Wikipedia] A cycloid is used by engineers and designers to make a roller coaster. In other words, it is a path that is followed by a circle on a straight line without slipping.
To determine the cycloid, you draw a circle and a line underneath it. Where the line and the circles connect mark point as p. The circle will spin clockwise. Divide the circle into equal parts. A circle has 360° if divided by 12 then you have each angle equal to 30°. Determine the center of the circle and from there following the line mark 12 equal points along the line and mark these from c_1 to c_{12}. Midway of the circle in the direction of the line mark midpoint as a first point c_1 then next point on circle outer edge c_2, then c_3, until c_{12}. Mark the 12 parts of the circle anticlockwise from 1 to 12.
In above given that the radius of a circle is r
Theta (θ) is the angular displacement of the circle then the polar equations of the curve are $x=r(\theta-\sin\theta)$ $y=r(1-\cos\theta)$
A tangent touches the outer part of the circle.
I will elaborate more on cycloid and prediction later in the report

to explain that the attacks were carried out by someone very intelligent belonging to a cult, I think the second Beast's cult. But who is this Beast?

At Gresham College, Christopher Wren was involved in experiments with magnetism. Through the study of the moon, he helped construct the telescope 35 foot (11m) high. These instruments magnified distant objects and made them appear as if near to you. The idea here is that of predicting the future. You can see the future now through his work. In other words, his work forecasted what would happen in the distant future. This is paramount to this report as I am going to show you that someone very intelligent manipulated others to pass a strong message and extract money from the economy for the benefit of the cult. In Revelation 13v 11-17 it is stated that the second beast will manipulate others and make sure that everyone has a mark on the right hand or forehead or some serial number. These indicate that the person belonged to the cult of chosen ones. These people were given secrets and tips to buy and sell and take money that is needed for the cult.

Christopher Wren's De Corpore Satrni.

Interesting here is Christopher Wren's written work about astronomy, especially the study of the planet Saturn. Wren highlighted the Oval shapes of Saturn: This was an analysis of the different forms of Saturn. Somehow, we see the same studies happening 347 years later but now it's the study of Satan the devil with the death of nearly 3000 people when his 'Death Trap' building ideas are incorporated into the Twin Towers.

The oval shape of Saturn.

The oval shape of the white house is derived from a ceremony known as a levee. In America, a levee is a tradition that was borrowed from the English law that was used as a formal occasion with the aim of introducing powerful citizens to the President. [9/11 could have invoked the levee ritual.] Characterized by formal dress, powdered hair, silver buckle-sets would visit the white house and enter the oval room. The president would be inside waiting by the fireplace. The invited guest would walk to

the president. The guest would bow. The presidential aide would announce their names to the president. The guest then returned to his place in a circle. After 15 minutes the doors are then closed. The president then walked around the circle before addressing everyone by name. He would bow down as well but never gives a handshake. After rounding the circle, the president returns to his place and stand by the fire. An aide would then give an instruction then one by one the guest would go to the president and bowed before leaving the room. George Washington ordered these bowed walls. Thomas Jefferson saw the idea of the levee as a way of going back to the colonization era by the British and abolished these. George Washington never occupied the White House as he was in Pennsylvania as the White House was under construction. Wren went on to study mechanics which deals with forces on objects and motions of objects. He learned about Isaac Newton's theories, who defined that force of an object is the mass multiplied by acceleration? He learned about gravity.
Christopher Wren as an Architect.

Very ambitious, Wren embarked on architect designing buildings. As mentioned above a week after submitting his design for St Paul's doom the Great Fire of London occurred. We know he went to France Paris with an architectural delegate and learned about Baroques. It is interesting to note also here that he might have had a vested interest. He stood to benefit if London was on fire. We know that by the 5th of September he had already started drafting new plans for London even though the fire was still burning. That raised questions about his motive and any involvement. Of all the people he stood to benefit. We know that after the fire even though his ambitious plan for London was not adopted nevertheless, he was commissioned to build 52 of the 87 churches. That was serious money over a short period. That raises questions; Could he have started the fire considering that he was poised to gain from all this?
Sister Cities or Twin cities.
The idea advanced after the second world war to foster

understanding and cooperation among different countries that were formerly enemies. The idea to encourage reconciliation. The history between London and Newyork goes back to the pre-independence around 1665 to be exact as developed in Volume I of the book. I advanced the idea that the London Map after the fire was incorporated also in the Newyork plan. In this volume, I am going to show the links and the impact these had on 9/11 and what it means. Today it is acknowledged that Newyork city is a twin sister city of London.

The Royal Exchange 1666 London.

This was founded in the 16th century by a one Thomas Gresham at the suggestion of a one Richard Clough who was an agent of Queen Elizabeth I. The idea was to make it the major place for the exchange of goods and services in London. Things to note here are that it is trapezoidal. [We know World Trade Center Building 7 was trapezoidal too.] The building designed was influenced by a Beurze or exchange market. The idea was first developed in Belgium by a one Van der Beurze. In London, the stock exchange started operating in 1668. Of interest to this report is the fact that it was occupied by Lloyd's Insurance market.

Royal proclamations at the Royal Exchange.

Traditionally the royal proclamations were carried out here on the steps outside the Royal Exchange. Announcement were made by a Herald or a Crier outside the Royal Exchange. The crier would dress up in a red and gold coat, white breeches, a tricorne hat, and black boots. Normally they carried a handbell and shouted Oyez, Oyez, Oyez! In order to attract people. Oyez means hear ye. Listen up! In England, the crier's main role was during public hangings. [Reminiscent of people screaming looking in horror as the planes hit the towers before they are died]. Here he would read out loud why the person was being hanged for and helped to cut him down or her. A practice common in England at the time. After hanging, people would be drawn and then quartered. That is their body cut into pieces before being displayed. It is true also that these town criers brought bad news such as tax increases and therefore were not liked by the people. As such were protected by law and could not be touched. Whatever they did was in the name of the monarchy. I have elaborated on this point regarding the divine right of kings and the prophet's role in the bible. The kings were believed to be sent by God as such were to be viewed as representing the wishes of God. No one could stop them. Stopping them would be like stopping God himself. Here on a human scale, we see the same concept being played here. The crier as a messenger of the monarchy is untouchable. A notion that will become clear as we progress. The designing of the building is important here. We know that its role was to act as an exchange with the center open. A place where buyers and traders would assemble. It is interesting here to note also that the Royal Exchange had a portico of eight Corinthian columns. On top of the columns is a semicircular top called a tympanum. Above this is an interesting quote from the bible. Corinthians written by Paul the Apostle. It says:

"The Earth is the Lord's, and the fulness thereof,"

This is a quote from the bible from 1 Corinthians 10v28.

But if any man says unto you, this is offered in sacrifice unto idols, eat not for his sake that shewed it, and for conscience's sake: for the earth is the Lord's, and the fulness thereof:

But Paul the Apostle quote the verse from the old testament from Psalms.

Psalms 24v 1-10 A Psalm of David.

The earth is the LORD's, and the fullness thereof,

the world and all who dwell therein.

2For He has founded it upon the seas

and established it upon the waters.

...

7Lift up your heads, O gates!

Be lifted up, O ancient doors,

that the King of Glory may enter!

To understand what is going on, we must go back to the original verse at the beginning. This is in Psalms 24. This verse declared that the earth and everything in it belonged to the LORD. The whole world and everything in it belongs to the LORD.

Meanings and background to this Psalms 24.
The Temple Mount is a hill in Jerusalem that is considered as holy
a place where God's House was supposed to be built. The first
temple was built by King Solomon the son of David. This First
Temple was destroyed by the Babylonians in 586 BC. These are
today's Iraq and Syrians.
King David wrote the music version of Psalms 24 after buying the
Temple Mount. The Jewish books with all laws, philosophies, and
thinking were called the Talmud. These books provide proof that
when David's son King Solomon visited the Temple, he was not
allowed even though he had brought the Ark of the covenant. He
was only allowed because he mentioned his father David. In
verses 7-10 we know Solomon had been denied access, and it
seems the song (psalm) is a kind of warning to those who had
refused to allow his son that they may be lifted to heaven. It
suggested that the people must recognize the highness of the lord
suggested by the 'lift up your heads.'
Interesting is the fact that if we go back to 1666, we know
Christopher Wren designed a plan of London after the fire. I have
also highlighted in the first volume that the king at the time had
showed dissatisfaction with the way London was at the time
before the Great Fire. We know that he complained about the
narrow streets and the overcrowding. Things he might have
attributed to the spreading of the plague. I have illustrated that
the king himself escaped to the countryside to Salisbury. If he is
king, surely one would expect him to have power over everyone.
Having that in mind we note that he could not do anything about
it. Probably the landowners refused to give away rights to their
property which is a very feasible explanation. Okay, let's assume
King Charles II after the Anglo-Dutch wars realized that he had no
money but wanted to rebuild the city of London. People like
Samuel Pepys had condemned the way London was at the time
like a slum with haphazard streets and overcrowded houses and
streets. He then expressed the desire to rebuild. He then asked
the people to relocate so that he can rebuild but they refused. We
know too at the time that it was a law that whoever destroyed

someone's house had to replace it. We know that meant a lot of houses and a lot of money too. The Royal Navy of which Samuel Pepys was one was being paid in debt vouchers, so King Charles II had no money to relocate the people or rebuild their houses. I explained in detail too that the kings believed in Divine Right something that gives them great powers over men. Powers not to listen to any men. So, given that situation, we would expect the King to just take the houses and land and rebuild the city. So, we ask why he did not go ahead. Okay, money was a problem but that alone cannot explain this. It makes sense if we consider what happened to his father Charles I. The king Charles I his father was hanged, drawn and quartered because he believed that kings were sent by God and therefore answerable to God alone. He believed in the divine right of kings. His son Charles II we can only assume that fearing to end up in the same shoes as his father he didn't take things into his own hands. This is supported by the fact that he commissioned the designing of several blueprints for the city of London just after the great fire of London 1666. We know also that he faced stiff resistance from the owners of the land and buildings that have been destroyed as the new plans advocated for a new change and uses that meant relocating people as well. We also know that the insurance claims took time to process as well. Most of the plans were deemed as unfeasible and therefore rejected. It is also special to note that one of the people to submit the plans for the new London after the fire was Christopher Wren discussed above. His ambitious plan for London was rejected as unworkable for the reasons explained above. One thing that is interesting here to note is the fact that his blueprint first is like Newyork city as indicated in the first Volume. But of great importance here is the fact that the plan looked like an aerial view of the Temple Mount and its surrounding that is the Temple of Jerusalem. One of the oldest places in the bible. Mind you this Christopher Wren was a highly educated man. According to Wikipedia: He was

"an English anatomist, astronomer, geometer, and mathematician-physicist, as well as one of the most highly acclaimed English architects in history. [4] He was accorded responsibility for rebuilding 52 churches in the City of London after the Great Fire in 1666, including what is regarded as his masterpiece, St Paul's Cathedral, on Ludgate Hill, completed in 1710."

He was educated at the University of Oxford. So, given that information, we know for sure that he knew the bible, the history of Jerusalem and its architecture. Why? We know that he is responsible for the designing of 52 of the 87 destroyed churches. We know churches and anything to do with this originated from the books now called the bible the oldest book in the world. So, he knew about the temple of Jerusalem. Another important point that he knew the bible is the fact that he submitted designed for St Paul Church Dome that had been dilapidated and that needed rebuilding. Yes, he designed the dome of this church called St Paul. The designs he did were submitted on 27 August 1666 just a week before the Great Fire of London. We know also what this Cathedral he designed meant. This was a church by one of the apostles of Jesus Christ. To understand my arguments, first, let's look at the Cathedral in question the one redesigned by Christopher Wren.

This was built during the gospel years from 1087 to 1314 at the site of the Ludgate Hill. This Cathedral was built and dedicated to the apostle Paul from the bible.

According to Wikipedia Christopher Wren and others didn't like the way the Cathedral was built. It had old Gothic-style features, and the tower was not up to date with the times as Wren puts it. He wrote in his 1666 Of the Surveyor's Design for repairing the old ruinous structure of St Paul's:

It must be concluded that the Tower from Top to Bottom and the adjacent parts are such a heap of deformities that no Judicious Architect will think it corrigible by any Expense that can be laid out upon new dressing it.

[Wikipedia]

Interesting here is the fact that Wren had proposed to destroy the Cathedral tower and replace it with a more modern Cathedral that reflected taste and modernity, but this was rejected by the clergy and the citizens of London. Wren went on to request that he replace the tower with a dome but offered to preserve the Gothic building of the cathedral. I must emphasize here that this Christopher Wren was adamant that a tower was not good and as such should be replaced with a doom. This will make sense when we consider the actor playing Christopher Wren in our script. Namely Larry Silverstein. Assuming our script is based on London 1666 we can see why it would make sense that Larry wanted the towers gone. We know that they were old, and occupancy rates were very low. They had asbestos as well. Going back to 1666 we know for sure that Christopher Wren had been appointed the King's Surveyor. He now had the authority of the king and was being paid by the king. He had changed professions so many times and most of his previous works had nothing to do with the king. Yet we see him announcing every project he embarks on to the king but because most had nothing to do with the king, he did not get the recognition he wanted. He realized that the only profession that can link him to the King was architecture, land, and buildings. We know that his neighbor Samuel Pepys was a king's man in the Royal Navy. We know life was hard even the king's Royal Navy staff at one point were being paid in debt vouchers. So far, all his profession had no lucrative income. He spent time at the Royal Observatory researching. This is a job respected and with an income and prestige too. Just one week before the great fire he was proposing plans to rebuild the tower of the temple. Which he did and replaced the tower with a dome made of wood. Just a week later everything was on fire that means redesigning again as he had wanted. If he was being paid for all these things, then he might have had a huge motive to see the city burning so that as the King's only Surveyor he can get a lot of money redesigning the whole city the way he wanted and getting credit as well. The method he proposed here of removing the tower is of great interest here. According to the 1666 Of the Surveyor's Design; the tower was to be removed from within to avoid damaging the surrounding Gothic building that was to be part of the new cathedral. Why was this Christopher Wren so much interested in the cathedral? We know that from the bible where the idea of this cathedral in question was taken that the cathedral especially this one was an equivalent in the form of the Temple of Jerusalem. This temple in the bible was a very holy place as illustrated above a place built by King Solomon as a place of worship. We know that King David wrote Psalm 24 a song in relation to this temple. This was an especially purpose-built building. It was like the vault of the modern-day bank. It was to house all important documents and wealthy of the people of Israel in the form of the Ark of the Covenant. A contract between God and his people the Israelites. We know that King Solomon brought the Ark of the Covenant there. This was made of gold. We see the same again happening in England. When the fire broke out people removed their valuable assets and took everything to the cathedral. A place just like its bible equivalent was believed to be very safe and strong to resist the fire. This was true but we also know that before the fire this Christopher Wren replaced the strong tower formerly build of brick and lead with a dome built of wood with the result that to everyone's surprise, the cathedral caught fire too mainly because this same Christopher Wren had left the scaffolding made of wood there that helped the fire to spread. Everything including the people's belongings and masses of stock was all destroyed. We know even before the fire Christopher Wren had proposed to change the cathedral to reflect modern-day architecture at that time, but he had to face stiff resistance. We can also deduce from Psalm 24 that we know that King Solomon was denied access to the temple he read or reminded the people the threat his father David had said in this song. Analyzing Psalm 24 it makes sense that it's a threat, not just an empty song. The king David knows that his son might face resistance. Why? This is because at that time it was believed that kings were anointed that is appointed by God. Kings at that time were chosen by God. God would send a prophet to choose the one to rule among them. We know as shown in Volume I that David was anointed by a one Samuel who was a prophet of God.

The prophet proclaimed that God had chosen this man to guide the Israelites. When Solomon his son had become king, he faced resistance simply because he became king through inheritance if you like instead by appointment. Therefore, even though he is king because he is the son of a king very few see him as appointed by God himself. David anticipating things he writes not a song but a threat. Psalms 24. The whole earth belongs to the Lord and everything in it. God through the king had established it and if you refuse to open the gates to my son, then you will all go to heaven. That is raised up. You will all be killed and go to have. The people had refused to open the gates to Solomon the king. So, do quote a song or warning written by his father. In other words, he is saying open the temple gates for me before I order you to be killed that is lifted up. It's a threat; open or you would rather be lifted that is ascended to heaven so that I can enter when you are all dead. This makes sense too in this situation. We see Christopher Wren's demands being rejected by the clergymen and the citizens. This Christopher Wren was originally from the Bishop's side these were in most cases against the kings. This is simply because the kings were corrupt. They would steal from the poor, oppress the poor and get involved in big lavish spending at the expense of the people. We know this because Wren's uncle Matthew was a bishop. The bishop's role was to worship God and guide the people and at the same time act as leverage between the king and the people. They were there to reduce the King's power so that he can't abuse his position. Now we see King Charles is now playing a power game. He appoints this Wren as a King's Surveyor with Royal authorization to act as a Herald or Crier. The people are refusing his demands to change the buildings and the cathedral. His building was built in the name of the Apostle Paul. Him as a learned person I think he knew about the world of the apostles. This is true because we see him advocating to replace a tower with a doom. We know that from the bible that the apostle preached about Jesus and his main work of Jesus was the teachings leading to his death. The betrayal and the last supper. Jesus's impact. We know Jesus had twelve disciples representing hours of a clock. We know he sat on the table and they all sat round around him, making him the 13. We get the idea of a circle that is doom. In English doom represent some terrible death or destruction. We know that the memories of the death of the king's father Charles' I by hanging were still in the minds of the people. Probably the fact that the king appointed Christopher Wren as his Surveyor to investigates not just the land but also the people's views and allegiances to the king. Wren as a very educated man he goes on to change the safest place and a place that housed all precious assets they had. A place that people had placed so much faith in. The idea here is that after the death of Charles I his father the people no longer looked up high to the king. The king was killed by a man. Most had a role in the church as well. The focus changed from king to church. This is true considering that Charles I himself associated himself with the church. Religion and monarchy went hand in hand I think it's true today as well. The time before the hanging of King Charles I the king was looked as high up like a tower. In Psalms, we know that during King David's time the king was a representative of God as king David was appointed by God. His son only became king because he was David's son. As such people relied on much or gave more respect to God's temple. He had chosen the temple and we see the same here. When Charles I died, and the monarchy was abolished people needed something to look up to. The king is dead so what do we do? We build God's temple with a tower that goes up. King Charles II after being restored realized that things are not the same anymore. People are paying too much attention to idols. The tower of the church. This is not just architectural no. The king feels people spend time worshiping towers looking up to towers on top of the cathedral instead of him as was during his father's glory days. So, he devised a plan. Why not destroy that tower in which people are putting too much faith in maybe they might start listening to me? Solomon has the same problem, but he relies on the song or words of threat written by his father. Wren is doing the same. Destroy the tower replace it with the dome sending a clear message. In a week the whole city was destroyed. This is to the advantage of the King. Now the king had a duty to rebuild everyone's house. That way people would no longer look up to the tower. But they would look up to the king. The one who had built them new houses. Now the king slowly gained his place among the people. It's the restoration of faith and trust in the kings. His father's death had shattered any trust in the kings. His job through this Wren was to put conditions in place so that the people would no longer look to idols or towers for help but to the king. God has sent a plague to kill all, but the king would eliminate the plague but there must be doom first. For any new beginning, those who refuse will be lifted to heaven. If that happens the king will have access to all the properties and land you are refusing access to. So, a threat not just a song. Christopher Wren's use of gunpowder to demolition the cathedral cemented together by the molten lead.

The fire according to Christopher Wren

"caused 'the spreading out of the walls above ten inches from their true perpendicular', up to the last fire, of which he says; 'The second ruins are they that have put the restoration past remedy, the effects of which I shall briefly enumerate."

[Sancroft's letters.]

Christopher Wren the King's Surveyor declared that the "King [had] issued an order in council for taking down the walls at the east end, the old choir and the tower, and for clearing the ground in order to lay a fresh foundation."

While the destruction was being down Christopher Wren was designing the new cathedral preparing sketches. In making notes Christopher Wren noted that whoever had built the building in the first place had not put strong and enough pillars to hold all the heavyweight on top. The foundations around the pillars were not strong enough. The soil at the bottom was marshy and the number of people who frequently visited the cathedral meant weakened foundations as well. He noted that the pillars were too light to hold all the weight on top. To prevent the collapse of the spire-the top roof of the cathedral, he ordered some timber, and the tower to have bands included in it and "braces of iron wrought by anchor smiths who were accustomed to a great work for ships."

Use of the Plummet.

What is a plumb bob or Plummet? This is a raised weight that has a pointed tip at the bottom. This is used as a reference line called a plum line. This was used in surveying. The idea being to establish a nadir to determine gravity in space. The nadir is the point at which the sun or moon is directly below you on the other side of the earth. The opposite is the zenith which is above. In other words,

"the nadir at a given point is the local vertical direction pointing in the direction of the force of gravity at that location."

[Wikipedia]

Figuratively it is used to reflect the lowest point of a person's emotions. The original instruments were made of lead. The plummet was used to determine the center of gravity of an irregular object.

"In figure drawing the plummet is used to find the vertical axis through the center of gravity of their subject and is used as a reference point." [Wikipedia]

Christopher arranged for a Plummet to de dropped from the highest place on the spire that is the roof. He reckoned the best height to be 123 meters. He ordered the dropping of the plummet to be repeated and each time noting the speed of decline. We know also that Christopher Wren had leveled the streets of London marking and designing streets as the King's Surveyor. He had advanced a map of London to the king even before the fire of 1666. The state in which London was at the time after the surveys before the fire made Christopher Wren doubt that there was any chance that London could be made one of the most beautiful cities in the world. Wren noted that London had dark crooked streets. Smoke was a problem; sanitation was a problem. The houses were all built of wood and the streets were narrow. He noted that the contagious plague was still prevalent during his surveys before the great fire.

Factors hindering implementing Christopher Wren's plans.

We know that even though Christopher Wren had designed new plans for London, the plans were not implemented. A lot of factors made the whole process cumbersome. The following points are noted by Wren himself. He wrote that the problems were unmanageable:

I] The people would disagree with any plans to displace them; huge quarrels usually occurred.

ii] Fear of change was a common problem. Moving away from their site was something not welcome.

iii] Wren noted that the need for speed if the project is started, was a major problem as winter was around the corner. If a project was started, it had to be finished before winter.

Iv] Another problem was that the city authorities had let the houses for short-term leases of 7 years making any building of the city difficulty.

A quick note here is that Christopher Wren himself was happy after the fire of London in 1666 which he regarded as a blessing from God as he had more ground to work on that resulted in speed development, improved sanitation, better houses built of stone, wide streets, and above all the plague was destroyed after the Great Fire of London the plague did not return for 200 years.

As I have argued above, I think it's open to arriving at the conclusion that everyone with the responsibilities of putting things right namely the Mayor, the king, and the king's surveyor had wished for the fire as a solution. That was to erase all the problems raised by rights to land. The fire as an accident would simply mean compensation to the owners as covered by insurance rather than negotiations to part away with their rights to land. That would speed up things as well as the rebuilding would commence soon after the land has been cleared of the burnt remains of the fire.

Personal circumstances that might have contributed to Wren's hard work.

When all this was happening Christopher, Wren was busy planning a wedding to a Faith Coghill his wife, and they got married in December 1669. That might have explained the ambitious plans. Wren needed a lot of money. From doing voluntary work with experiments to be the king's Surveyor just how much one would get paid for designing the whole city? We understand he ended up rich. Looking at the person playing his role in our script the reconstruction of the 1666 London Great fire Larry Silverstein we can see that 3 years after 2001 the battle for the $billions started in the courts. Christopher Wren was responsible for the building of the Royal Exchange on a larger scale. King Charles II laid the first stone as the building commenced in other words his work was given a Royal seal. After building the city after the Great fire some builders still used forbidden materials and practices, this angered Christopher Wren who then writes to the king asking him for permission. He writes: "May it, therefore, please Your Majesty to issue a royal proclamation, to put a stop to these growing inconveniences and to hinder the buildings which are not already or shall not be licensed by Your Majesty's grant; and effectually to empower your petitioner to restrain the same or other ways to consider off the premises as in Your Majesty's wisdom shall seem most expedient." [Wikipedia]

The king then went on to consider the petition in council and then grants a proclamation giving Christopher Wren full powers. Wren now with the powers given unto him by the king went on to make sure that no one was breaking the rules and using wrong materials.

It is interesting to note here that there were suggestions to completely rebuild the cathedral even before the Great Fire of 1666. Wren was one to advance such suggestion the time he was asked to repair the building suggesting that building a new building would be better. After the fire one, Dean William Sancroft is believed to have acknowledged that Christopher Wren was right after all that a new building was the answer. After the fire destroyed the cathedral, some walls were still standing but regarded as dangerous and had to be taken down. The problem was that the walls were held together by the molten lead that had melted during the fire. Christopher Wren to bring down the remaining walls used the then-new technique of using Gunpowder to demolition the remaining stone walls covered with molten lead. This was an experimental technique and as a result, a lot of people were killed, this was due to be uncontrollable nature of gunpowder. Several of the workers were killed. Neighbors heard noises.

In 1669 Christopher Wren becomes a member of the Honorable Artillery Company. In 1673 Christopher Wren gave up his membership of the Savilian astronomy professorship. Abandoning his research work of the moon to the study of dust and turmoil. It is in the same year that he tried to rebuild St Paul's cathedral, but a wall and rubble were left proving difficult to remove as stone were fused together with molten lead. The remaining structures and walls were very strong and hard to pull down. Christopher Wren as a founder of the Royal Society a scientific organization given the king's seal by Charles II wanted to use what he had learned at the Royal Society into practice in solving problems. Samuel Hartlib who was a neighbor of Samuel Pepys the diarist and John Evelyn the diarist was a member too of the Royal Society. At the Royal Society, Christopher Wren had learned how to raise weights by use of gunpowder. Gunpowder was used to blow up houses during the great fire of London. Wren advised the use of gunpowder to blow up the central wall that was 60 meters high. Some men used pickaxes at the top and those below would use shovels to remove the broken walls. Wren came with a gunner from the Tower of London. He asked the men to dig a trench. This was near the north-west pillar. He created a space in the wall of 2 feet square size at the foundation. A box with 8kg of gunpowder and a fuse was inserted in the hole and some gunpowder poured into the trench all the way to a safe place away from the tower. The gunpowder was lit. Christopher Wren used 3,6 kg to bring the north-western wall down. This raised 3000 tons of weight up, but no damage was observed on the wall. This is very interesting as will be discussed below. This passage will be read in line with Psalms 24 or 1 Corinthians 10v 28 that reads; "the earth belongs to the LORD and all that befall it. Where threats, as I explained, were hidden behind the song that Looks up to the Lord if you refuse you will be lifted. Here we see 2996 nearly 3000 lifted to heaven. Just like in our script the fall of the towers through the use of thermite a form of gunpowder was used. Aluminum from the planes and iron from the jet fuel. Christopher Wren blew up the north-western part of the tower with 3,6 kg of gunpowder lifting 3000 tons of weight. This excited him that he ordered a repeat of the same process of using gunpowder. This time though he had to go out of the city leaving the second officer in charge. The second officer wanted to set a record that he increased the amount of gunpowder. This made stones be thrown everywhere during the blast nearly injuring the bystanders. This forced Christopher Wren to devise another method.

The Battering Ram.
After the destruction and panic the second gunpowder blast caused Dean Sancroft, a city representative refused any more blasting leaving Wren resorting to the use of the Battering ram that was 12meters long. He got the idea from the bible in Ezekiel when one was used. Like the plummet, it had an iron spike. In old times this had a huge timber at the middle with triangles surrounding it for easy carrying by at least thirty men as the one designed by Wren. The ram itself was attached on top of the roof of the building and the men half on both sides would swing the ram from side to side until it has gained momentum and velocity to destroy the wall. On the first day, the wall did not fall only to fall the second day.
At Falcon Inn at Southwark Christopher Wren built a little house that had red bricks. This building acted like an observatory place where he observed the cathedral's progress and the other building in the city. We know too the man playing him Larry Silverstein built World Trade Center Building 7 with red masonry bricks. This was designed as a time-ball as shown in the first volume.
Retractable Pillars or Column or trusses of the World Trade

Center.

Christopher Wren witnessed Sir Isaac Newton's retractable telescope. An idea that might have been incorporated into building the World Trade Center Building 7 by Larry Silverstein could explain the free fall. The retractable pillars could be held in place with pins that could be pulled causing the building to free fall.

Christopher Wren always paid on time his Royal Society fees that in the end he was reelected a member of the council. We see Larry Silverstein taking a 99 years lease with $10 million paid monthly on time. Gaining special privileges with the Port and Authority of Newyork.

The Script Role of Larry Silverstein who is playing Christopher Wren.

There is no doubt that Larry Silverstein is the perfect actor to play Christopher Wren's role. In real life we find Larry Silverstein walking Christopher Wren's life road doing most of the things he did as we shall see the only difference is the scale of the activities. Construction of 7 World Trade Center.

Larry won a lease from the Port Authority of Newyork and New Jersey to construct a red building called the World Trade Center 7. In our script, the idea is that Christopher Wren is a role model or a godfather of Larry Sliver-stein. We see Larry Silverstein getting ideas from the life of Christopher Wren. We know that Wren was fascinated by astronomy. We know that he constructed and or modified the telescope and most of the time would look up into the sky to study the moon. In comes Larry he shows enthusiasm when he learns that the Port Authority was leasing the World Trade Center the tallest building, high up into the sky towards the moon. Wren before the 1666 great fire of London had a problem of redesigning the city first because of the short-term lease of seven years offered by the authorities. Larry knowing this gets a 99 years lease and just like Wren paid the monthly fees to the authorities on time and this won him favor with the local Port Authorities when most could not pay on time.

Dissatisfaction with the current building.

Just like Wren Silverstein showed dissatisfaction with the current Towers that he proposed to replace these with new buildings. This is true that just like Wren Silverstein's strategy was to destroy the old building and replace it with a new building. This is very true with Wren during the St Paul Cathedral assessment. He wanted a new design, but he faced still disapproval from the local clergymen and authorities. The above account has shown a clever and intelligent Wren putting to test all the things he had learned at the Royal Society. In the lab, he had experimented with gunpowder to demolition buildings. He had contributed to Isaac Newton's laws of gravity. We know he had used a battering ram to destroy the walls.

Silverstein was learning from Wren to solve current problems in our script. We know that Christopher Wren attempted to destroy and lift 3000 tons of rubble to the sky and displace the building. It is clear that Christopher Wren used 3,6kgs of gunpowder. He dug a trench and made a box hole in the building and poured in the 3,6kgs of gunpowder. He inserted fuse dynamite and poured some gunpowder in a trench to a safe blasting place. Far away he lit the gunpowder and watched what happened. The gunpowder blew up and displaced 3000 tons worth of rubble into the air. Pleased he realized he would save time and money as this might have taken months to demolition. Excited and about to carry out another blast the King summoned him to go to Salisbury for surveying duties leaving his second officer a one Tom Woodreff. We pause here. Is it not surprising too that we find the same method happening on the 9/11 attacks? Okay. We saw a plane Flight 11 crash into the north tower. Here the tunnels are in the air and our gunpowder is in the form of the airplane kerosene and thermite that will form from aluminum and iron oxide in the fuel. Comparison between Gunpowder and Airplane's (Thermite source).

Gunpowder also known as black-powder consists of potassium nitrate, sulfur, and charcoal. It has incendiary properties in that it can be used as a bomb. It generates a large amount of heat and gas volume and because of this, it is regarded as a propellant. But of importance here is the blasting power that it is considered as a demolition agent. Gunpowder is regarded as a propellant. The propellant is used in the production of high energy that energy is used in the movement of the gas or fluid. The movement manipulating Newton's third law causes the propulsion of an object. Thrust is generated that in turn pushes the object forward as an equal force is exerted in the opposite direction. Gunpowder is considered as a low explosive meaning that when burning it burns at supersonic speeds. It is used in gun making where its ignition results in a force being generated that pushes the projectile at enormous speed. In shattering rock, it is a bad choice because of a low-yield explosive power. This was 400 years ago when Christopher Wren used the gunpowder to demolition a building. Nowadays technological advancement has meant new cost-effective methods of blasting much better than gunpowder. Our script shows Silverstein learning from Wren's mistake. Surely there is a better propellant out there that can do the same job. Thermite.

This acts the same way as a black-powder or gunpowder and is an incendiary element that is it can be used in the making of explosives and bombs. We know that airplane frames are made of high-grade aluminum and that the planes carried jet fuel nearly 18 000 gallons between them. Thermite is a composition of aluminum oxide and iron oxide which is rust. The aluminum is used as the reactive metal. The World Trade Center Towers were 28 years old meaning the presence of some form of rust. Aluminum as the best reactive metal.

i] It is the cheapest of the highly reactive metals.

ii] It has a low melting point of 660'c meaning it can melt other metals. This means it turns to a liquid that corrodes other metals faster.

iii] It has a high boiling point of 2519'c which means any reaction involving it will reach a very high temperature causing massive structural damage especially in the demolition of steel structures.

iv] Reaction causes a low-density characteristic of aluminum meaning it can float on top of steel and iron causing it to disintegrate and succumb best for demolition steel buildings. Thermite reactions burn extremely high with what are called exothermic reactions. Reaction produces high temperatures up to 2500°c molten liquids that can easily consume steel.

The best thing with thermite is that it has its own oxygen supply meaning the fire will keep on burning at high temperatures. Exothermic Reactions.

This is any reaction that produces energy through heat. Sparks are realized as small molten iron that ignites surrounding areas as well-meaning setting up the fire fast. This reaction gives energy to its surroundings. The energy needed to initiate a heat reaction is much less than the energy realized. The major advantage or ideal attribute of thermite is that it burns even in water.

In short, thermite is an explosive and works on a small area at a time spreading rapidly producing very high temperatures within a short period. Thermite is used in cutting materials in welding. Thermite is used in the military to make hand grenades and in the destruction of steel structures. Thermite has been used to destroy the heavy artillery weapons made of strong steel and iron. Small streams of iron are always produced during a thermite reaction. Jet fuel itself is a propellant itself based on the combustion of kerosene. This is a hydrocarbon used as a fuel.

Okay back to what happened the day Christopher Wren used gunpowder to demolition St Paul's Cathedral and what happened on 9/11. We know that initial demolition by Wren moved up to 3000 tons of rubble in the air. The second blast was overseen by the second officer when Christopher Wren was summoned by the King to go to another city to survey the land. It can here also be inferred that since he was pleased about the initial results, he could have wished to add more gunpowder to blast the building down but scared or just to cover his back and reputation of the king he worked for as a surveyor he might have left knowing that the second officer would do what he can't do. Above all, any damage was not attributed to him or the king. We know Larry Silverstein was not there as well at the towers even though he was supposed to be there. We know Flight 175 struck the South Tower at 94-98 Floors. Inserting kerosene from the jet fuel with almost 69% iron oxide and the planes providing the aluminum that is needed to form thermite which is an explosive as detailed above. A product that has incendiary properties that is it is used in explosives and bombs. In both cases, the methods are the same in that both gunpowder and thermite acts the same way and thermite being a better alternative. Christopher Wren as a member of the Royal Society did extensive studies of gravity having his work reviewed also by the great Isaac Newton who discovered the law of gravity. Christopher Wren used a plummet in surveying and in the demolition of the building. This was a great way of pulling the building down using gravity. The above building on top of the impact level was to act as a plummet that would force the buildings down Just like in his experiments one of the buildings the North Tower was impacted at an angle at nearly 45 degrees angle. This caused a structural imbalance with weight on one side causing the top floors (pointed plummets) to fall even faster and quicker. We know also that the second officer after Christopher Wren had been summoned elsewhere by the king, increased the amount of gunpowder with the result that debris flew everywhere causing damage everywhere.

Why Christopher used the gunpowder and why whoever is behind 9/11 used the thermite and fuel.

We know very well why Christopher used the gunpowder. It was fast and cheap, and he was excited to experiment as well. We see in our script Silverstein employing the same methods with the same effect that a building that was supposed to take months or years to demolition the proper way is taking just 56 minutes and 102 minutes, respectively.

Motives of both Christopher Wren and Larry Silverstein's Actions. Both men were very enthusiastic and excited to rebuild the city to reflect what they wanted to see as part of the modern architectural development. For Wren, this was a newly attained profession that had, at last, brought him close to the king as the King's surveyor. We know for sure even before the fire that destroyed London in 1666 including the St Paul's Cathedral that Wren had designed plans already. We know he had replaced the tower with a doom based on the temple of Jerusalem. We know too that he had submitted the plans for the redesigning of the cathedral and had done the doom replacing brick and stone tower with a wooden doom signaling already it's doom. To make things even worse, he left a wooden scaffolding surrounding the cathedral that was made of brick and lead adding wood that can easily burn upwards to the lead-roof. Work was finished on 27 August with the fire starting on the 2nd of September 1666.

ii] We know he had faced stiff objections from the people who hang onto their land making his plans infeasible. The people had refused to relocate or sell. Most also had lease agreements for seven years making any giving up or building difficult. I think the same was true at the time with the World Trade Center lease tenants. He would have wanted to develop a much better building that increased occupancy rates.

iii] The country had been through a second Anglo-Dutch war in which it lost. Money was scarce. The year before that a plague had killed 100 000 just in London. This is true, we also know that Newyork had suffered the 1987 stock market crisis with the results that during the 1990s the buildings had fewer occupants rates the main reason that the Port Authority of Newyork and New Jersey decided to lease the World Trade Center. All the 1990s nothing changed. It is true most floors were unoccupied. Still, Larry Silverstein was paying more than $10 million per month.

iv] At the time we know too that the King had reputation issues that the people were not listening to him. He had escaped to the countryside to Salisbury. Above all his father took things into his hands thinking he was God's messenger and as that can do anything ending up being tried and killed. The king used the Christopher Wren of a bishop's origin through his uncle Matthew Wren to gauge the people's views. Kings at that time would simply order or command changes, but after the death of his father Charles II was very cautious. I can only infer that he used clever ways of threatening the people. He replaced the tower of the church with a doom. After the death of his father Charles I by hanging the monarchy was abolished. At this time people looked up to God that was portrayed by the high tower on the cathedral before that they looked high to the king. When the monarchy was restored, I think it was a deliberate move to destroy the tower. The king had returned people needed not to look up to God but to the king who was appointed by God as his representative. Larry Silverstein wanted to rebuild too. Replacing the towers with modern buildings but I can only assume too that people might have refused to cancel their leaseholds. The political climate was not good as well. We know George W Bush's popularity was low. We know he was elected with lower votes with the issue of Florida. His unpopularity was due to his father's record too during the Iraq wars. The mayor too was very unpopular.

v] Christopher Wren's use of gunpowder displaced 3000 tons of rubble in air blasting everything into pieces. In the 9/11 attacks, 2996 people were killed.

vi] Christopher Wren redesigned the whole city and we know he redesigned the Royal Exchange and constructed this too. On one of the columns was an inscription that is originally from the bible and it reads.

"The earth is the Lord's, and everything in it."

This is a verse from the bible from 1 Corinthians 10v26

The cathedral he had redesigned and repaired was in honor of the apostle Paul in the bible who visited Corinthians and preached there. We know at that time people did not believe that a king was a representative of God after the crimes of his father. During the time of King Charles II, the king faced opposition from the people. His authority was low and approval ratings low as well. The plans designed by this Christopher Wren were rejected as people refused to give up their land. The cost of rebuilding also meant stiff opposition. The verse he used is found in Psalm 24v1. We know that it was written in the time of King David. In volume, I know king David was appointed by God through a prophet after being selected to be king as a young man. At the time kings were

regarded as divinely selected by God. People subscribed to the divine rule. When he died his son, Solomon became king. Here he was king simply because he was a son of a divinely appointed king and as such, his authority was questioned and doubted by the people. King David anticipating the struggles of authority his son might face when he is dead composed of songs in the book of Psalms. These songs were threats, especially this verse used by Christopher Wren.
Psalms 24v 1-10
The Earth is the LORD's
A Psalm of David.
The earth is the LORD's, and the fullness thereof,
the world and all who dwell therein.

7 Lift up your heads, O gates!
Be lifted up, O ancient doors,
that the King of Glory may enter!
We see King Solomon being refused entry into the Temple he had built by the priests and the elders. He then quotes the same verse written by his father king David. The verse reminds the people that the earth belongs to God and as such, him being the son of God's servant King David and as such everything belonged to him too. So, if everything belongs to God whom he represents why were they refused him entry? It does stop there. People at that time just like in Christopher Wren's time had lost faith in the kings. The kings were cruel and abusive to be representatives of God who is believed to be good. The people now placed faith in the church in temples or cathedrals which are houses of God. We see towers that go high up to God now being built as part of all God's houses. In psalm 24v1 the people now look to the towers and house of God instead of from the king. The verse then pleads with the people to look up to the king so that the king can be honored as the king and be accepted. The verse then threatens that do you prefer then to be lifted up first so that the king can freely be accepted when you are gone?
verse 7

Lift up your heads, O gates!
Be lifted up, O ancient doors,
that the King of Glory may enter

...

acknowledge the king or be lifted up.
This is a threat that; would you prefer to be lifted that are being killed? This is true as this is used in the ascension to heaven of Jesus Christ. So, king David is using this verse to threaten the people: accept my son your new king or be killed that is be lifted to heaven. We see the same scenario too. King Charles I was dead after being hanged for treason and his son King Charles II is having difficulties to be accepted as the rightful king. We know too that he is weak with no powers as the people challenge him reminding him too about what happened to his father. He approached the people and declared that they give up their land for development. They refused and can only do that if the king would pay them more for their land. As explained above he had no money. He was paying the Royal Navy with debt vouchers. He sent one of them, from the bishop's circles; who were responsible for the church and acted as elders with voting powers. Just like King Solomon king Charles II is having the same problems. Wren being Clever as he was warned the people. The change has been set already signified by the changing of the tower of the St Paul cathedral with a doom made of wood. A clear message that the people are doing worse by looking up to buildings (idols) instead of looking up to the king. Your doom has been devised to listen to the king or the fire will bring you doom. We replaced the strong stone and brick tower with the wooden doom. Listen or be lifted. A week after this the whole city is burnt down. Now the people who were demanding huge compensation claims from the king must wait for a year for the courts to decide. Everything now is in the king's favor. The land is free, and rebuilding can start straight away. I think this could mean that somehow, he might have warned the people. That could explain why so few people died due to the fire itself as only six deaths were recorded. In the 2000s we see the same situation. George W Bush is in the same shoes as first Jesus

Christ himself, King Solomon and King Charles II of 1666. The people are not listening to him. People are conspiring to bring him down. This is true as we heard Donald Rumsfeld declaring that this guy was not fit to run the administration. He was leaking a lot of money in the tunes of $2,3 trillion. The people in government were trying to bring him down. He escaped the pentagon the following day. We know Charles II escaped when faced with problems going to the countryside.

Blackmail with intent to provide Protection making the kings and the President Protectorates.

Someone in this situation is in real trouble. We have seen this in the bible with the same happening to Jesus with people doubting his authority as sent of God and not just that but charged of blasphemy a charge that carried the death penalty, we have Judas Iscariot setting him up and selling him. The same is true as people criticized Charles II for abandoning them. We have people accusing George W Bush of incompetence. I think it is at this time that someone especially the second beast discussed above, took things into his hands. He saw an opportunity to making protection deals with the leaders concerned. Bush is at his lowest point called the Nadir. At this point, we know people have no way out and can agree to any deals that can retain the previous status quo. I think it's at this stage that evil steps in. Someone with the knowledge of the activities of Christopher Wren, Charles II, and the bible kings. This person took advantage of their weaker situations and guaranteed to protect them at any cost and in return, they had to obey certain demands.

Protection Contract. (Fictional Scenario).

I think for argument's sake let us say the second beast (Beast II) then stepped in. He then said to Bush.

"Look. I know you are in deep trouble. As things stand, I think you have no chance. Your career is finished and there is a great possibility that you will end up in jail too."

"I know they are blaming me what did I know? I have no idea where the money is. I think it's because of this obsolete system.

It's the 2000s yet we are still in the paper era. The dot.com nearly crashed that should make the electronic transaction possible."

"I know but what can you do now?"

"Nothing. I am finished even though I did nothing wrong."

Bush looked sad and hopeless.

"They are after my head,"

"I can help."

Bush looked surprised but not excited.

"It will cost you your family and your children,"

"I am not sure about that. I don't want to be a slave you know."

"It's not that bad. This is what I will do. I will erase all your problems overnight. Give you another chance. Make everyone respect you. Give you the best approval rates. Guarantee your next term after this. I will be responsible for your external problems and all international affairs."

"What do you mean? No. I am a leader of the Superpower nation how can you portray me as weak. I would rather die than take a dip."

"Leave everything to me. I will be very secretive. I have all the answers. I know they will try to trace all this. Your problem is the financial records. I know your central financial buildings are the towers. We destroy them to erase all the paper trail." Bush quickly gets up.

"No, I can't do, they are the symbols of American pride. After all, they are always people there a lot of people. No, I can't."

"Listen they are your problem. The system they are based on is obsolete. We destroy them we cause financial record's structural damage that makes fraud efficiency."

"Hold on. What Fraud? I did not take any money."

"I know." Beast II replied calmly.

"So what fraud are you talking about?"

"I was referring to Froude efficiency. The more impact we introduce the greater the output."

"Still makes no sense."

"Okay, I will be honest with you. I am the Beast II from Revelations 13:11-18

The Beast out of the Earth.
11 Then I saw a second beast, coming out of the earth. It had two horns like a lamb, but it spoke like a dragon. 12 It exercised all the authority of the first beast on its behalf and made the earth and its inhabitants worship the first beast, whose fatal wound had been healed. 13 And it performed great signs, even causing fire to come down from heaven to the earth in full view of the people. 14 Because of the signs, it was given the power to perform on behalf of the first beast, it deceived the inhabitants of the earth. It ordered them to set up an image in honor of the beast who was wounded by the sword and yet lived. 15 The second beast was given power to give breath to the image of the first beast so that the image could speak and cause all who refused to worship the image to be killed. 16 It also forced all people, great and small, rich and poor, free and slave, to receive a mark on their right hands or on their foreheads,17 so that they could not buy or sell unless they had the mark, which is the name of the beast or the number of its name.

"See to carry out our tasks we need a lot of money. One of your head is injured and your term in office is about to come to an end. The seven heads represent the number of years you will be in office in full command. But we see your years are numbered you could be out of office. I speak like a dragon and we know what the dragon is good for."

"Breathes fire. No, I am not going to buy that. Fire kills you know."

"Let me finish. I will be under you and listen to all your requests and demands without any questions. I will make everyone on earth worship you. Everyone at this stage knows that your head has been damaged, and I can heal you give you back your position as the president. I will perform great signs even if it means everyone seeing fire coming down from heaven. I will let the whole earth witness such an event. I will manipulate and deceive all. I will make everyone look up to you again as they know you are finished when they see you back in the pentagon, they will be shocked and fear you thereby command your respect. I will restore and make your image and approval rates better. Those

who refuse to honor you after your new image must be killed. All
ask is that you give me permission to give everyone a mark."
"A mark? What mark?"
"I will need you to construct a transparent wire compound that I
will hold indefinitely. After some time being confined in small
places, they will develop medical issues and then we give them
the 'English honey'."
"You are not making any sense."
"Society Collapse Disorder! I will treat them like honey bees. We
put them in a man-made beehive. We see the impact of removing
the male workers. I bet the local community after some time will
collapse and financially, we cripple them too. If no money, then
it's easy for them to do what we want. The idea is to replace the
expensive white sugar with the English honey. Like I said after
some time fear will weaken them and they will do everything we
say. Then and there we start giving them this English honey that is
marks or tags with serial numbers. We will be able to control
everyone. Those who have the marks and serial numbers will be
part of us in our cult. They can buy-and-sell. The idea is to provide
our cheaper 'English honey'. Everyone with a mark will be able to
do what we want, he or she can vote for you."
"Sound exactly what I want; some respect and honor from these
people just like my father had. What is in it for you?"
"I got most of what I wanted."
"Eh and what is that?"
"The $2,3 trillion and all your future. You will be mine. You are
now like a person on death row. The clock starts when you agree,
how long it takes depends on you."
"Son of a bitch! You stole the money. I better kill you myself."
"That's how I operate. That is what is called Protection. I get what
I want. I set you up, so you don't refuse. Now it's up to you. Face
your mates who will do-a-Jesus on you or subscribe to me. Join
our cult. I don't take anything from you. I restore you as the
President. I listen to all your demands. If someone gives you pain
just point him to me, I will kill with fire from heaven just like that.
Just overnight the people will have forgotten about all this and

you know what they will give you the best approval ratings of any president."

"Impossible. You know I am the only president to enter the white house with very low votes. If it wasn't for Florida, I might not even be president."

"You have nothing to lose. I have a simple plan. I tell everyone to follow you and live or deny and die."

"Simple as that?"

"Yes. You need to respect and honor. You can only get that if you are serious. Why feel pity for people who don't follow you. Get rid of all those who oppose you so that your presidency is smooth. Would you agree?"

"True. I agree."

"You are in this situation because they are not listening to you. Correct?"

"Yes true."

"It's simple to find out who listens to you and who follows you. Whoever follows your lives. Whoever does not follow you perish. Fair. That's how you will restore your reputation. People after that will follow and listen to you."

"What should I do?"

"Let Donald Rumsfeld tell people to avoid high buildings and not come to work but to spend time with their kids."

"Why Donald Rumsfeld? If I am the President should I not be telling them that myself?"

"See, how then can you tell who listens and follows you?"

"What do you suggest then?"

"Let Donald figuratively tell them in a clever way. Those who understand are good for you. The rest are dead to you anywhere so why do you care?"

"I don't want blood on my hands."

"So, you are not a great leader like your father. Everyone listened to your father. The best President of all time."

"Okay, what must I do?"

"Tomorrow after the announcement leave the pentagon and go to an elementary school. Spend time there."

"Bullshit I think you are trying to weaken me further. You stole the money now you want me to go and spend time with kids when I should be in the White House. Do I look like Jesus to you spending time with his disciples instead of running away?"

"Now that you mention that that's the only test to see who follows you and commands your respect. Anyone who does what you will do tomorrow is your follower worth to save. Those who don't follow you let them perish."

Bush stood up and looked outside the window.

"I know you are scared. To be honest, your fear only points to your weakness. If it is in a war would you not save your men by leading by example? Sample principle here."

"If you agree then we have a Protectorate arrangement."

"I just cannot the USA is the most powerful country in the World. We are a superpower. I would rather go down than take the whole nation with me."

"I guess I just let them do you a-Jesus. This Protectorate certainly does not have to be in public news you know. It can remain a secret."

"America is capable of protecting its borders and our protection is the best. We go and defend others worldwide; it would be an embarrassment to us for people to hear that we are being protected by you. After all, we can protect our borders. In that regard, I say no thank you."

"I will still do some work on your family when you are dead or in jail?"

"Are you threatening me?"

"For $2,3 trillion oh yes. You know what I can get chips who can do you for nothing. I will do an an-Eisenhower. Done by your president during the 1960 incident. You see my goals are commercial and strategic for the whole world."

"There is no way congress and parliament would agree to protection. Taking us back to pre-1776. No way."

"If you know what I can do with $2,3 trillion you would agree with either way you are going down. I don't want to see you go down for something I can solve. This is an Amicable Protection."

"We are the mightiest country."

"Are you sure you can protect yourself from terrorists?"

"What terrorists? Internal terrorists can't justify protection."

"I know. I will do an Eisenhower and outsource as well as internationally. That justifies protection. When that happens fear will be written in the hearts and minds of all those who had witnessed this. People will wish they were the ones buried by the towers. For the next two years, everyone shall look to the sky in fear and all shall run away from the Towers or tall buildings. That way all the people shall look up to you. That is if you agree. People will no longer put faith in objects idols, or tall buildings but all men on earth shall look up to you. They will come to you and sit on your feet and embrace you. They shall ask for your help. They shall ask you to protect them. Whatever you will say no one shall object to. You shall go to war and no one shall object to that. You shall be feared. No one shall look to the sky too. Mankind's focus shall be on you. God has given us the power to act on his behalf for two years as in Genesis 3v22. We are like God now. We shall kill just like God does. I shall do like Christopher Wren and lift up 3000 tons of rubble to heaven. In doing all this I shall fulfill Revelations 13 verse 11-18. I shall give you protection and on that day you and those who listen to you shall know that I am the second beast and as such, I am the real superpower and not the USA. Tomorrow I go to school as I said. Moment of truth. If people listen and follow you, doing as you do then they shall be saved. The more people listen and follow the less the death rate. We can only find out tomorrow what these people feel about you."

"I don't know about that."

"Listen I will make a deal with you. If 5 people stay away from places of work out of a possible 3000, then you don't need my protection. But if you have less than five people, then you must become my protectorate. You will have all your freedom and you are responsible for your internal affairs. All external forces will be under my wing. All international negotiations and ventures will be through me. I have experience with these things so I will lead and guide you. Wherever you go, I will go. Whatever we make I will give you a cut too. My objectives are purely commercial. We will use terrorism to make sure that no national shall nationalize oil wells. That $2,3 trillion is money you might end up using on oil resources for the next 5 years. Money, I need very badly for that 'English honey' project."

"Honey Project?"

"Yes, we talked about this. You will name it the Guantanamo Bay Project. The purpose is to reduce resistance when we embark on our war on terror. That will weaken people. Seeing their brothers in compounds with no chance of getting out held there indefinitely will soften any resistance. This is a physiological mind game. Gods are clever and I will manipulate and do whatever it takes to win. Above all, we will need to give everyone on earth a mark through medical devices and this is the only way they will agree to such things without knowing. It is called taming. We will simply say being put in a cage over such a time will make you require such an implanted medical device."

"But you are never going to do that to everyone there are billions of them worldwide. How are you going to accomplish that?"

The Beast II laughed.

"That's when you come in. That's why I will spare you and protect you. You get everything you want I get what I want too."

"I know but you have to tell me?"

"Do you know that in 1662 4 years before the great fire of London on the otherwise of the world in Virginia a law was passed that children in the colony were born with the status of their mother? A Roman law called Partus Sequitur Ventrem "meant that the children of slave women were born into slavery, even if their fathers were free, English and white." [Wikipedia]

"I am not following. You talk about slavery which was abolished centuries ago."

"I know. We are going to use 'English Honey' to the women and all the children they will have. The children born to these women will have the status of their mothers and we don't want them to claim the same status as their fathers. That way we can be able to mark all of them. Give them serial numbers and tag all."

"Sounds bad what if they revolt? Things like this will always have a bad ending."
"I know that's where you come in. Anyone who becomes too big for his or her shoe is terminated."
"You think that is easy?"
"No, but you are going to pass the No Child Left Behind Act."
"How do you sleep at night?"
"Are you in or not? Any of those vetted to present problems in the future. All those who disobey will be killed at the same time as their father, but the world does not need to know this."
"So, tell me exactly in advance what I will be needed to do."
"Okay. Tomorrow depending on your leadership skills, we will see if 5 people can follow you. If that happens you won't need our protection but if less than 4 survives then we will take over. We restore you. You shall fulfill and implement our War-Contingency-Plan. Under the disguise of terrorism, we shall invade Iraq and denationalize oil wells. You will get your cut after the fall of Saddam Hussein. You shall put a new system. We shall destroy the towers. They are obsolete anyway this way we shall cause a trigger of the collapse of the markets in a few years to say six years depending on the damage to be done tomorrow. The money taken out of the economy will with other factors determine when the world economy will collapse. This will destroy all financial records and shall act as a trigger to the inevitable collapse. This will give us an opportunity to take more money from the world economy for giving marks to billions of people. You shall establish Guantanamo bay that will act to weaken the people and send a fear that we mean business to rescue our people dying too. We shall do an Eisenhower and send spies in the form of delegates to investigate for Weapons of Mass Destruction."
"Wait a minute it sounds like it's you who is making WMDs in the form of this so-called 'English Honey'."
"We need an alibi. We shall simply say they have WMDs after getting what we want who will care about all this. Trust me seeing their friends in cages like monkeys doing nothing with no chance

of coming out will make them shiver with fear."

"You sound like you have a manual on how to do this?"

"Let's just say we have been here and active for a very long time."

"What if we can't get the approval for a war?"

"Don't tell me your approval rates have been this bad?"

"It was hard even at the beginning they think I am just a daddy's boy. No one believes I am the president of the United States."

"Maybe we have to push them even more."

"What do you mean?"

"Break Nasser! That will make everyone support you."

"I can't do that?"

"Do you want, or you just go down tomorrow? Listen we are like gods and the more we kill the more we unlock the gates to longevity. Did you not read Genesis 3v22?"

"I don't believe in God."

"Me too but hey, we are the gods on earth we do what God would do. That means after all this with our ties laid down by Eisenhower a lamb will be given to us so clean and pure to sacrifice. This lamb is willing to kill his son for God. But we know there is no God. So, if he wanted to kill and sacrifice his son to God and if we are the Gods would that not mean that he is sacrificing his son to us. So, if he is willing to kill his son for us what stops us from killing his son too?"

"I don't know about killing sons. Are you saying that his father sends his sons to destroy buildings pretending to be terrorists so that he can move in and reconstruct the buildings? Are you saying that terrorism is a cover for his father's construction business?"

"Don't worry it won't happen on your soil so you will be fine. No one will give a fuck. The great Eisenhower showed us away during the 1960s I promise it shall be okay. Don't forget his father owes us $7 billion. I don't think you would want his son or grandson taking that money from us, do you?"

Bush did not reply but got up and walked to the window and stood there looking outside. The time he turned to look at the Beast II, the beast had already gone but he could hear its horns from far away. The following day a few people stayed away from

their places of work to be precise only 4 people out of the target of 3000 people followed the example of the President of the United States and only these listened to the president.
"We surely have a lot of work to do." Said the president slumping down in his chair saddened that no one followed his example.
End of a fictional scenario.

CHAPTER FOUR

Timeline of 9/11 events.

7:59 am.: American Airlines Flights 11 and Boeing 767 carrying 82 passengers and crew members depart 14 minutes late from Logan International Airport from Logan International Airport in Boston, bound for Los Angeles International Airport. Five hijackers are aboard.

8:14: United Airlines Flight 175, a Boeing 767, carrying 56 passengers and 9 crew members, departs 14 minutes late from Logan International Airport in Boston, bound for Los Angeles International Airport. Five hijackers are aboard.

8:14: Flight 11 is hijacked over central Massachusetts, turning first northwest, then south.

8:20: American Airlines Flight 77, a Boeing 757 with 58 passengers and 6 crew members, departs 10 minutes late from Washington Dulles International Airport for Los Angeles International Airport. Five hijackers are aboard.

8:42: United Airlines Flight 93, a Boeing with 37 passengers and 7 crew members, departs 42 minutes late from Newark International Airport, bound for San Francisco International Airport Four hijackers are aboard.

8:42–8:46 (approx.): Flight 175 is hijacked above northwest New Jersey, about 60 miles northwest of Newyork City, continuing southwest briefly before turning back to the northeast.

8:46:40: Flight 11 crashed into the north face of the North Tower (1 WTC) of the World Trade Center, between floors 93 and 99. The aircraft enters the tower intact.

8:50–8:54 (approx.): Flight 77 is hijacked above southern Ohio, turning to the southeast.

9:03:00: Flight 175 crashes into the south face of the South Tower (2 WTC) of the World Trade Center, between floors 77 and 85. Parts of the plane, including the starboard engine, leave the building from its east and north sides, falling to the ground six blocks away.

9:28: Flight 93 is hijacked above northern Ohio, turning to the southeast.

9:37:46: Flight 77 crashed into the western side of The Pentagon and starts a violent fire.

9:45: United States airspace is shut down.

9:59:00: The South Tower of the World Trade Center collapses, 56 minutes after the impact of Flight 175.

10:03:11: Flight 93 was crashed by its hijackers as a result of fighting in the cockpit 80 miles (129 km) southeast of Pittsburgh in Somerset County, Pennsylvania. Later reports indicate that passengers had learned about the World Trade Center and Pentagon crashes and were resisting the hijackers. The 9/11 Commission believed that Flight 93's target was either the United States Capitol building or the White House in Washington, D.C.

10:26-28:22: The North Tower of the World Trade Center collapses, 1 hour and 42 minutes after the impact of Flight 11. The Marriott Hotel located at the base of the two towers is also destroyed.

10:50:19: Five stories of part of the Pentagon collapsed due to the fire.

5:20:33 pm.: 7 World Trade Center, a 47-story building, collapses. The last supper and the betrayal.

Two days before the festival of Passover the scribes, the chief priests and the elders of the people nonstop searched for ways to bring Jesus into custody to kill him. Judas Iscariot betrayed Jesus. The Passover is a day that people celebrate the liberation of the Israelites from the Egyptians. This is reminiscent of 10 September 2001 with George W Bush being accused of incapable of running his administration. I suggest too there were some conspiring among the people in government conspiring to get Bush. That could explain why he left the pentagon going to be with his disciples the students the kids of the elementary school. The announcement by Donald Rumsfeld that $2,3 trillion was missing from missing from pentagon could have been calls to get him arrested. In this script, George W Bush is playing Jesus Christ. One of the security guards at the elementary school on 9/11 whispering (selling him or identifying him) in the ear of George W Bush could be the one playing Judas Iscariot.

1 Corinthians 10v 26.

"The earth is the Lord's, and everything in it."

The important thing to note about this verse is the fact that the verse does not say God but the LORD.

A lord can be:

"An appellation for a person or deity who has authority, control or power over others acting like a master, a chief or a ruler. The appellation can also denote certain persons who hold a title of the peerage in the United Kingdom or are entitled to courtesy titles. The collective "Lords" can refer to a group or body of peers. [Wikipedia]

Considering the fact that the Royal Exchange was built in England where they call peers as Lord. Using this sense of the word this can mean something else and the verse could mean.

The earth is the LORD's and everything in its meaning belongs to those who have been granted peerages. I am saying this because since the 1600s the Royal Exchange was built with this inscription that:

"The earth is the Lord's and everything in it."

First, before we go deeper can we look at an important concept referred to as protectorate.

Protectorate.

A protectorate, in its inception adopted by modern international law, is a dependent territory that has been granted local autonomy and independence while still retaining the suzerainty of a greater sovereign state. In exchange for this, the protectorate usually accepts specified obligations, which may vary greatly, depending on the real nature of their relationship. Therefore, a protectorate remains an autonomous part of a sovereign state. [Wikipedia]

British Protectorate.

The idea of a protectorate is common among the British where British Protectorates have been around for a long time. The British Crown exercised sovereignty jurisdiction. The country had its own rulers, but the crown made treaties and negotiated agreements. The protectorates were therefore ruled indirectly. The British advisers oversaw taxation and international relations.

Implementations.

This was implemented sometime in 1763 by King George III of England who used his Royal Proclamations. What he did is provide the basis for making treaties with North American people. The king saw the need to be domineering in the whole region providing protection to all the territories. Any country as such was to be called a protectorate.

When the British took over Cephalonia in 1809, they proclaimed, "We present ourselves to you, Inhabitants of Cephalonia, not as invaders, with views of conquest, but as allies who hold forth to you the advantages of British protection." [Wikipedia].

A lord is a person who has power, authority, and control over others like a ruler, a master, etc. In modern-day, the lord is used to refer to peerage especially in the UK. Peerage is ranking in a society based on hereditary ties. There are five peer ranks.

Duke

Marquess

Earl

Viscount

Baron.

The Barons are addressed as the lord, but they are too apart from the Dukes. The upper house of the Parliament of the UK is called the House of the Lords.

Implied and not expressed Protectorate.

In order for protectorate ideas to work the country that will end up protected must have been a weaker country or a powerful country but one that is suffering external attacks that it can't control these external forces on its own. This is true that is why you see the rise of terrorism something that is an external entity unable to be controlled by the country concerned. These are mainly external forces that will give rise to the need for a protectorate agreement implied or expressed. Somehow also this saw the rise of terrorism in recent decades the only factor that warrants the idea of a protectorate. We see even powerful countries like America with all kinds of power and weapons unable to protect themselves from the effects of terrorism. This factor makes America not the most powerful country in the world. Why? Simply because even though America declares itself to be a Superpower in the world that is it is the most important and powerful country in the world it is unable to protect itself. We have seen that the USA defends a weaker country or does something regarded as an act of a superpower and following that certain events at home then expose them to the world that even though America claims to be the Superpower it is not. It still suffers from external attacks. That is the main reason why all attacks and horrific events experienced by the USA since declaring itself as a superpower are carried out mainly by foreigners. That means there is another superpower out there never to suffer from foreign attacks. This superpower can give America protection whether implied or expressed. We see often America suffering from horrific external attacks. To those who understand this America is definitely not the Superpower. A Superpower never suffers from external attacks. Okay, it might experience an attack and all these attacks are internal only home-grown dissatisfaction leads to these attacks and are generally viewed as trivial acts. The idea is to maintain the idea of a Superpower. A Superpower just like God has three main characteristics defining it. These are that it is omnipotent, omnipresent and omniscient. Omnipotent.

This means all-powerful. A country such as that has supreme power. This country has power over nature and everything and controls everything. The idea here is that of abundant power. Although other countries like the USA declare itself as the most powerful it is also a fact that it is one of the countries that suffer horrific events that throw the idea in question. This is true and those with deep insight will understand that to them the USA is a laughingstock in that regard. Wait hold your thoughts! This is not disapproving America as the "most powerful" the fact I am portraying in this report is an almost all-powerful country. This is in line with the fact that powerful countries reflect the image of God; a superpower. The idea I advanced in the first book. The idea arises from a deeper understanding of the world. Something God did not want people to grasp.

Genesis 3:22 King James Version (KJV).

22 And the Lord God said, Behold, the man has become as one of us, to know good and evil: and now, lest he put forth his hand, and take also of the tree of life, and eat, and live forever:

[King James International Bible]

It's knowledge that is beyond the mere understanding of world events. I think if you are to ask people today which country is the most powerful today, most would say the USA. But after you acquire a deeper understanding, you will find out that the USA might be the weakest country needing the idea of a protectorate simply because it is a country easily attacked from internal and external sources too. That alone gives it an image as being a weaker country and as such cannot be regarded as the most powerful or the supreme power. Again, hold your thoughts. My point is that a Superpower one, near to the gods, one that has grasped the true knowledge referred to here cannot be viewed as such and experience attacks like that. Therefore, it can't be an omnipotent country. In the first Volume, I advanced the idea found in Revelation 13 that of the beast.

Revelation 13 King James Version (KJV);

13 And I stood upon the sand of the sea, and saw a beast rise up out of the sea, having seven heads and ten horns, and upon his horns ten crowns, and upon his heads the name of blasphemy...

7 And it was given unto him to make war with the saints, and to overcome them: and power was given him over all kindred, and tongues, and nations.

8 And all that dwell upon the earth shall worship him, whose names are not written in the book of life of the Lamb slain from the foundation of the world.

9 If any man has an ear, let him hear.

10 He that leadeth into captivity shall go into captivity: he that killeth with the sword must be killed with the sword. Here is the patience and faith of the saints.

11 And I beheld another beast coming up out of the earth, and he had two horns like a lamb, and he spake as a dragon.

12 And he exercised all the power of the first beast before him and causeth the earth and them which dwell therein to worship the first beast, whose deadly wound was healed.

13 And he doeth great wonders so that he maketh fire come down from heaven on the earth in the sight of men.

We see this is the definition of a Superpower regardless of the fact that it is good or bad. This is the idea advanced in the world especially now. Some countries understand this, and some have ranked countries based on this notion and to some extent, this has given rise to the idea of a protectorate. An idea I will address in detail and highlight why there is a link between this and the problems in the world including terrorism. So, we know God acknowledged that some humans have acquired a deeper understanding of life in the world and as such he saw some of these replacing him. Doing exactly what he can to an extent that he delegates his duties to them but just for a short period as an experiment to prove a point that okay. I understand you, humans, you have eaten the fruits. Yes, you now have the knowledge like a God, and you are like Gods in the fact that you can now live forever as long as you feed that means killing people as God does. An act that has the sole purpose of correcting the earthly balance. This person or country is feared by everyone on earth just like God. A powerful country commands everything earthquakes, floods, gravity, diseases you name it and that makes people run away. God will never be attacked by anyone no matter what. Such a person who can't be attacked is a Super-person. Imagine a person who encounters a savage killer like a lion. Surely you would not expect a reasonable man to stand and slap the lion. Any reasonable person will run for it. God simply is feared. The prophets in the bible hide and cover themselves in the presence of God. No one will ever think of attacking someone that powerful. All external forces will never attempt to attack that country. Such a country is true Superpower. Although that country can suffer from similar events e.g. those arising from terrorism, they are only local ones that are pushed aside as internal dissatisfaction to the local policies adopted. In that case, these are events for changing local policies rather than acts of terror to show who is the real boss. In this light, it is not shocking that although America believes itself to be the Superpower in this light, it is the weakest country. A country that others would view as needing a protectorate status. This is true we see a country that has experience in these matters always there on America's side guiding it and supporting it but in fact a daylight declaration to the world as to who is the real Superpower. In other words, Britain is seeking a protectorate agreement to protect America from external forces which it can't protect itself from. This is true with all terrorists' attacks on America by foreigners. That explains also why most of the evil acts are carried out by foreigners. Simply that is the only condition that can give rise to the need for a protectorate agreement whether expressed or implied. We see this is true throughout history. The pearl harbor attacks, the 9/11 attacks, the space shuttle Columbia crash, etc. are events by foreigners or external forces that America can't protect itself from. This indicates the need for a hidden Superpower like Britain to declare itself as a protector of the USA, although this is hidden or secretive as well. I developed this idea as the godfather-protégé, big-brother-little-brother notion, the master-student, etc. This is an implied protectorate status in that Britain cushions America from external forces but does not interfere with internal politics. Britain is a country that has the Superpower status in that it offers express or implied protection in the form of a protectorate to protect the USA from external forces. American cannot protect itself from external forces whilst the British cannot be attacked by external enemies although Britain suffers from the same events as terrorist attacks those in Britain are due to home-grown. This augments the idea that no man in his normal sense would slap a lion, but most would run for their life.

Omniscience

This is a very important concept. Knowledge makes one omniscience because if you know everything then you are very knowledgeable and very clever you don't need anyone to guide you instead you guide others. We know knowledge is associated with books. The only widely believed religions that have larger followings and religions associated with God or gods are religions with knowledge in the form of books. God and books in the form of the bible or the Quran. Those who want to be viewed as the Superpower associate themselves with books, written laws, information and have a collection of such dating back many thousand years ago. We have seen the English kings trying very hard to document everything so that they have the omniscience status, the knowledge of everything so that it is in a position to protect others. We have the Domesday Day as far as 1018 in England where the king requested the documentation of everything. We know too in the bible the prophets being asked to write down their knowledge into books. This means that this country is all-knowing meaning knows in great detail the past, the present, and the future. This country is the godfather if you like an idea advanced in Volume I. This country is the Superpower because it is just like God and will never be taken by surprise but knows everything happening around it. The knowledge here is total. Such a country is a Superpower because it can never be caught unguarded because someone within it knows what is going on around it. Such a country can go to another country and in broad daylight can offer protection to another country. We know the great fire of 1666 in London was documented by the kings "prophets' just like in the bible associated with God. We know also from these accounts that after the fire the major issue was terrorism. Although the plague had been the main reason behind the fire here when America was attacked, we see everyone declaring that they are external forces that are true but in fact, this can only prove that America cannot be a Superpower simply because the weak can raise hands at it. To fully understand the idea behind this, take a leader of the mafia or gang leader for example. No one touches him. The fact that no one lifts his hand at him, but all flee for their lives makes him the leader he is, otherwise, no one would follow him and as such he is the super-supreme leader of the gang or mafia. The fact the Saudi terrorists attacks America four different ways sends a message that America is not a Superpower and as such, there is another Superpower out there. Britain was the Superpower for a long time until the 1950s when its power started to crumble. This is true as in the 1956 Suez Canal incident. We saw America threatening Britain with sanctions and demanding that Britain and France pull out of Egypt something which was never heard of before. This elevated the USA as the Superpower of the world especially when Britain withdrew without realizing their goals for invading Egypt. In Britain, we saw terrorist acts in the 1600s with the Gunpowder Plot of 1605. I have covered this in the first Volume. Here we see the rise of terrorism directed at the state and their leaders by dissatisfied bodies, but these were local or what they called domestic terrorism. The 20th century saw a rise in external or export terrorism due to foreign policy and the war of the previous years. This gave rise to the need for expressed or implied protectorates.

Omnipresence.

This superpower has a presence everywhere. The country has an empire worldwide. Just like God is everywhere. This idea makes other countries want to dominate the whole world creating colonies and residency in other countries in the form of embassies and local representative and state companies everywhere. This also gives rise to the idea of protectorate or protection. The idea is that the country is trying to spread its wings so that it is felt and present everywhere.

Anti-colonization and the rise of protection and protectorate and implications to terrorism.

As time passed, the people of the world started realizing that colonization was a bad practice against the human rights of every man. We have seen the American Revolution and all the other revolutions that followed. The colonizing powers realized that this affected the omnipotent and omnipresent of their powers. Such they are no longer as powerful as they can be. They no longer control everyone. People and other countries have gained power and are now sovereign and as such, they don't need anyone to protect them or tell them how to run their countries. This is the idea behind the Anglo-French versus the American incident during the Suez Canal. The Americans threaten the Anglo-French pact with sanctions when they tried to re-colonize an independent sovereign country. America is a former colonial country of the British bitterly fought such a move of handing back the Suez Canal to western colonialists. British dominance was only through colonization and as people started to understand that there are human rights entitled to them, their grip on power and control started weakening. We see America rising to power simply because it recognized the idea of sovereignty. This signaled the end of the British power simply because it grew out of oppression and colonization. After the 1950s British status started crumbling and the empire crumbling. The only way Britain can remain a Superpower at the same time recognizing every country's sovereignty was through the idea of protection and protectorate. The idea here is that the British rulers would only have a commercial and political advantage and maintain the same position as during the colonial era when they had an empire was through the system of protection and protectorate. All the countries concerned would be responsible for all internal activities and leave foreign affairs and protection to Britain. Yes, the country will have its sovereignty, but all foreign affairs would be in the hands of Britain who will amalgamate their power and protect everyone. That still gives the British the Superpower status. But to protect another country that country must be unable to protect itself. This is true with small countries but how to control and even offer protection to bigger countries so that

Britain can still retain the power it had before the decolonization era. First, let's look at the rise of the idea of a protectorate.
The Protectorate.
"The Protectorate began in 1653 when, following the dissolution of the Rump Parliament and then Barebone's Parliament Oliver Cromwell was appointed Lord Protector of the Commonwealth under the terms of the Instrument of Government," [Wikipedia] Protectorate.
In this sense, the country in question has its own sovereignty but leaves its foreign policy and international relations to a protector directly or indirectly.
The idea behind this is the rationale.
I] Amicable Protection.
This is beneficial to the protectorate in the sense that the country protected is not expected to oblige to some demands. The protector protects out of the need to do that for a moral obligation or some strategic stance, for example, to stretch their power without demanding anything from the protectorate. In this case, the UK can offer to protect a poor country just to minimize the power of its rivals like the USA. The more people it offers protection without asking for anything the bigger influence it has. This is a strategic stance.
Colonial Protection.
This is similar to a colony in that even though the country is recognized as independent still the conditions are so bad that it makes the situation resemble those of colonization even though a country is regarded as independent. Hence the idea here is that of indirect rule.

Foreign relationship

In this setting, the country will only deal with the protector and the other countries will talk to the protector. In this case, all military activities are jointly taken between the protector and the nation concerned.
A look at the British Residency of the Persian Gulf will elaborate

on the idea of Protectorate and protection.
The British controlled several Persian Gulf states even after independence, the reason being a commercial one.

The Persian Gulf Residency. The Trucial States.

Britain persuade a commercial policy in the Persian Gulf because of oil. But to be able to control the countries in the region and offer them value for the oil something wrong had to happen. This saw the rise of pirates after the British rule (British Raj) was established in the region. The rulers ignored the pirates by the Qawasim who were members of the royal rulers of the United Arab Emirates. This caused the British to invade the Persian Gulf and ratified the once existing treaty called the General Maritime Treaty of 1820
This treaty was a result after the invasion of the British in the Persian Gulf killing some leaders there before agreeing to a treaty to offer protection to all Persian Gulf countries at the time in exchange of obligations namely to ban piracy, slavery, etc. The idea of such a treaty was to establish open links of communication between the British Raj; the Indian appointed representatives of Britain and the UK. After this invasion, the old treaty was rectified. Britain made an agreement with the Trucial rulers to seek consent from Britain when dealing with foreign nations. Britain assumed control of foreign affairs of most countries in the Persian Gulf. There was a shift from a purely commercial to a strategic goal that of acting as a Superpower. Britain then established its political objective by establishing an ambassador. This positioned the British as the protector of the Persian Gulf countries leaving the sheiks to deal with internal affairs. Very frequently the British would offer advice and deal with foreign nations regarding the improvement of their administration. These treaties helped the British establish a presence in the Gulf area and helped them carry out their extraterritorial jurisdiction roles.
"British extraterritorial jurisdiction in the Persian Gulf was implemented in accordance with the British Foreign Jurisdiction

Acts of 1890–1913, which empowered the Crown to establish courts and legislate for the categories of persons subject to jurisdiction by means of Orders in Council."

[Wikipedia]

What gave rise to the need for protection and or protectorate? In the Persian Gulf in the 1800s, we have seen that piracy and sabotage gave rise to the need to protect the Persian Gulf nations. The presence of external attacks gave rise to the need to protect the locals from external attacks leaving the nations deal with internal affairs while the British dealt with foreign piracy attacks. The British were in a better position to eliminate piracy as they can impose a blanket solution that covered the whole region rather than a specific country. That helped eliminate piracy. We saw that the British Empire declined after the 1950s with America becoming a Superpower. Terrorism increased as well as a regional or international threat. The 9/11 attacks and other attacks showed weaknesses of the USA and that discredit them as the real Superpower. Britain again rose from the ashes offering indirect or direct protection in return asking for different conditions. After the 1956 Suez Canal incident, the British sided with the French than with the Americans. The late 1980s to the 2000s saw increased attacks on the USA as they embark on international wars. That gave Britain a chance to offer the USA protection to help it go to war to fight these terrorists in return make America be its true friend. We saw Tony Blair declaring to go to war in Iraq side by side with the USA something you can call Amicable protection. The terrorist attacks have proved that the USA is not the day's Superpower. In fact, the USA can be regarded as the weakest and as such requires the protection of the experienced British. The British have seen all this. As omniscience, they have all the knowledge. They can just look at the Great Fire of London of 1666 and know what will happen and how to tackle the issue. Looking at World War II one can argue that the money Britain borrowed might have been protection money demanded implicitly by the British for protecting them against Hitler a threat to everyone at that time. That can be explained by the fact that Britain did not want to pay back the money. I think Britain believed to have charged the USA and Canada protection money for going to war. Britain only paid the debt after another expedition: invasion of Iraq.

It can be inferred too that Britain could have taken advantage of the American situation and saw an opportunity to provide indirect or hidden protection. We know that $2,3 trillion was missing from the pentagon something that would have meant the end of the career of George W Bush. Just like in Jesus' case we know the law-makers the elders and the members of parliament were conspiring to get Jesus arrested. Donald Rumsfeld's stance of pronouncing that $2,3 trillion was lost by pentagon could have suggested the need to act upon it by getting George W Bush into trouble at the same time showing that he was not capable of running his administration. We know that Jesus had no one to protect him with the result that he ended up dead. What if someone saw the opportunity and offer the President protection? Erasing the problem in return of certain favors that involve financial gains? Maybe a slice of the missing $2,3 trillion? This is a real possibility. We see George Bush abandoning the pentagon and going to an elementary school. A place of learning. Maybe implied agreement of the fact that he is a learner and can do whatever it takes to learn from this mistake and correct the error in the future. Or the person behind this the one offering him hidden protection saw an opportunity and took it. We know he was in serious trouble. I guess the members of parliament might have been calling for his head. The USA one can say that it is not a Superpower if its losses such an amount of money. Someone after seeing such an opportunity might have stepped in. Made the problem of the missing $2,3 trillion go away and actually give George W Bush a strong standing in the office and the highest approval rates attained by any president. But how? The person opened the manuals on how to solve such a problem. He opened the Domesday. Surely 11 September could have been filled with the talk of George W. Bush losing the $2,3 trillion had the attacks not happened. The person realized from the Domesday book (A manual with what to do when faced with a dome-like problem.) that a solution is there. He realized that one Charles II after the Anglo-Dutch wars were in a similar position in which his role was in question. Just like those days, a plague here in the form of the disease was prevalent. A problem only a fire can solve. He realized that a plague had affected the USA financial economy too, the only difference being that this disease was one of insider trading, cheating disobeying the Federal Securities laws, etc. causing the loss of such money. He realized that fire still was the only solution. He read more and realized that a one Christopher Wren was faced with a task to move a wall he used gunpowder to lift 3000 tons off the earth into the air. He noted that Charles II although he did not give the command nevertheless the solution worked. He proposed a solution.

Piracy and terrorism.

External forces like piracy and terrorism are the only grounds that can justify another country offering protection to another. These are the only activities that can weaken a country with a super-status position to be regarded as not such. How can you be the most powerful when you suffer the worst catastrophes? It makes no sense. Bear in mind the arguments I have advanced above about omnipotent, omniscience and omnipresence. That surely doesn't fit the criteria. In fact, America needs the protection of a real superpower in the definition I have advanced above. The only country fitting that criteria is Britain. Could this be sweet revenge after the 1956 humiliation of Britain by America or just a coincidence? The rise of terrorism gave Britain an upper hand and actually to those who know history for the past 2000 years makes Britain the hidden superpower the only question to ask is that: Is it by design, nurture or nature? If you think of terrorist acts instantly the Twin Towers comes to mind with nearly 3000 people to have perished. I think this image can make you feel the weakness of America and its inability to protect itself from external forces. Its problems are not internal but international hence the need to be protected by a real superpower that can deal with such external forces effectively. We see Britain with experience with the pirates of the Persian Gulf designing strategies to thwart such an attack. Hence making the USA a protectorate of British. The Columbia disaster as well can be seen as an incident that highlighted the need for America to outsource protection from external influence. The atmosphere, the space is an external force that can cause all kinds of problems with loss of life. Britain again knows how to deal with such a problem although the answer is figuratively in the form of a remark that "break Nasser" [break NSA] completely within six weeks. We see later George W Bush announced the end of the space race. Britain after all these atrocities in the USA realized that it can actually go it alone. It no longer needs the protection of the European Union that gave it protection as well in which we can infer that it was a protectorate of the EU itself. Now if it can be a protector of the USA why does it need the protection of the EU. If Britain can protect the USA, then it can be independent after all it has a well-documented history with problems and solutions. After all, it has experienced centuries ago everything happening now to some of these countries. The Germany killings of the Jews with carts full of corpses in and out of the cities although the deaths were caused by nature. It had experienced the great fire of London in 1666 and similar conditions to the 9/11 attacks.

The art of supply and demand.

I have advanced the idea that the need to be seen and recognized as a Superpower can be a trigger for a terrorist act. In the past international conflicts and politics gave rise to terrorists but as we know throughout history, these were nothing than domestic quarrels. A Superpower country is a country that dominates the whole world. Intervening to protect the weak and starting wars to dominate regions by eliminating opponents or showing the others who are the real boss. We have seen a rise in international terrorism linked to the idea of a Superpower. As the empires grow and spread to foreign countries so as the animosity and the threat of terrorist acts. The more you intervene in other people's affairs the more the attacks. We have these as the reasons given as the motives of the terrorists together with the unhappiness with USA foreign policy. This foreign policy is a direct result of the need to be seen around the world as a Superpower. But when there are two Superpowers in competition with each other fighting for the position, then it is not straight forward.

Competition to be regarded as real Superpower and terrorists' activities.

This can be said to be true that competition can lead to dirty tricks as in the airline's saga in the UK at the time in question around 2000. We saw the BA resorting to dirty tricks to remain on top when faced with the new and emerging airline that of Richard Branson. We saw stiff competition and the weakening of the BA position as it started losing customers to its rival with the result of unethical methods being employed. What if it involves two countries fighting for that number one position? Britain as an advanced nation throughout the report grew on colonization and oppression grounds. When the world gained a better understanding of their rights surely that meant the end of the British Empire. But still another option was available to them to enjoy the same status while acknowledging human rights. Britain had experience with pirates and sabotage and how to use this for political control of regimes and for expanding just like before. The only thing that can justify protection is the threat of terrorism. Terrorism can weaken a Superpower position to one of being a protectorate. This is true after the 9/11 attacks that Britain cemented the relationship it had with the USA from the World War years. 9/11 not only showed that America was weak and could not protect itself but also that it was not a Superpower as in the definition I have developed in this book. A Superpower in the real sense is like a god on earth see above comments about Revelation 13 and Genesis 3v22. God realized that some nations have become Superpowers like gods on earth. His only fear that man is made up of flesh and feelings (unlike him a spirit) therefore will experience too much pain if he is to act like God. He delegates his activities for a certain time. Such a nation is feared, and the thought of that nation being attacked is very remote. This also makes that country abuse others, kill at will, control the destination of others, intervenes secretly and get away with murder. Why? Because it is simply doing what God would otherwise do. Maintain a perfect balance by killing such-and-such people. Just like God, it creates situations to justify its protection. This takes me back to the idea of competition among two Superpowers one dying and the other just resurrecting. We saw Britain being dragged out of Egypt and threatened with sanctions by the US after the Suez Canal. We saw America dominating world events and showing the omnipresence but lacking the omniscience and the omnipotent to the extent that domestic attacks also increased caused by foreign terrorists a condition of paramount importance to justify the need for protection by another nation. Who do we see coming to America's rescue? Britain. You think you are a Superpower, but you are not, to be honest, you can do with being my protectorate. You can have your sovereign but when it comes to protection, I will guard you and advise you on how to deal with a terrorist. America attacks the mountains first when Britain was advocating for the invasion of Iraq. Britain did not hesitate. It knew what the cause was. It had experience with pirates in the Persian Gulf. Attack in Iraq. Still, the USA Refused. Tony Blair went on to cook the Iraq dossier. Still, the USA refused to invade without the United Nations' approval. Britain being clever knew that the UN was a body they created themselves and therefore was under them ignored all that. America still needed a push. Britain slowly took center stage as the Superpower guiding the scared USA. Despite Bush's approval rates going high to 82% after the attacks still he waited nearly two years before attacking Iraq. The only reason that made the US invade Iraq was another tragic-push the Columbia disaster on 1 February 2003. Two tragedies within a 3-year space was hard enough. We see a grief-ridden so-called Superpower now waging war. It happened again to us why can't it happen to others. Like I have advanced in this report and Volume I. The main reasons behind any Superpower activities fall into two categories. As strategy-gaining goals or for commercial advantage. Once again, we see Britain delegating all major activities at the USA and just a day after the death of their trophy; Saddam Hussein Britain as the Superpower was now spreading the proceeds of the kill and on 30 November 2006 paid America it's share for going to war with it disguised as a World War II debt. Britain indirectly and secretly took back its position as the real Superpower feared and recognized as such. Another look of how many countries still indirectly or secretly under the British rule can only show America as the Superpower by word of mouth but honestly a British protectorate.

Can America and Britain sponsor terrorists' activities to justify being a Superpower?

I think there is a lot to be said here. I have shown in Volume I that the presence of short- and long-term contingency plans influence the decisions taken and events associated with such decisions. In the 1960s we saw Eisenhower outsourcing activities to the British and seeking help from Pakistan to establish a base there to spy on the Soviet Union. Having said that little is left also that one can only say such a possibility is real. We have conspiracy theories arguing that the government ought to have known and or played a part in all this. The fact that protection something that the British advocates for, even today and since the 1600s is a fact even today only makes that a possibility. The fact that to offer this protection the threat of terrorist acts must be high and real and not imaginary cannot exclude such a possibility. In fact, there are reports that some governments fund terrorists to justify the need for protecting others. Like I have said the sole purpose of protection in this sense is commercial and strategic as a Superpower. It can be argued reasonably that the desire to remain on top as a superpower can make one country sabotage its rivalry and offer it protection making it a secret protectorate at the same time telling the whole world who really is the daddy; the boss.

CHAPTER FIVE

A Complex Hierarchy of Dubious Institutions or foreign Governments.
Presence of institutions that insures and spread risks literally in order to provide protection as a source of terrorist acts.
Imagine a world where people create problems themselves in order to provide you protection as a way of earning a living and making a fortune.
Spread of risk in insurance circles means an accumulation of risks from more than one source. First, let's look at the Lloyd of London normally housed in the Royal Exchange.

Lloyd of London.

This is a market for insurance where parties come together to join a syndicate and to insure as well as spread risk of different businesses and organizations. The syndicates are different, and they all insure against different risks. Lloyd's of London is an intermediary between brokers, insurance companies and clients. Buyers search for insurance protection against certain risks. Sellers representing people who sell protection negotiate on behalf of them. There are brokers as well who try to negotiate and leverage deals between buyers and sellers. A broker charges a fee for executing a buy or sell deal. Lloyd's of London is not an insurance company but a corporate body. This provides a marketplace to buy in syndicate groups governed by the Lloyd's Act 1871.

The Sasse Affair.

Sasse Lloyd's underwriter gave someone else its underwriting duties namely an unscrupulous Florida agency who in turn placed property insurance on dilapidated slum houses in downtown Newyork South Bronx. The properties were burnt to the ground and the people behind this then claimed insurance taking as much as $40million. The syndicate members refused to pay and instead sued Lloyd's for not supervising and doing its managing job.

Financial Crisis of 2007-2008

This started in the USA in 2007 in a subprime mortgage where the people could not afford to repay the loans before going global causing the international banking crisis. This resulted in the Lehman's Brothers filing for bankruptcy a once investment bank. Most of the investment banks were taking too much risk offering mortgages to people who would otherwise not afford to repay. The world financial system was poised to collapse, and something had to be done. The governments all over the world embarked on a global bail-out of banks to avoid a total collapse. Nevertheless, A great recession still took place. The European debt crisis followed.

Subprime mortgage Bubble.

The government relaxed the regulations through the anti-predatory laws of 2004 that meant higher lending rates. Securitas backed lending increased as well and the Community ReInvestment Act made it easy to lend to low- and medium-income families. The lenders saw a low risk as the subprime mortgages could still be bundled and passed over as low-risk securities. These bundles could be sold on too, in the end, they ended up at Fannie Mae and Freddie Mac who went burst.

Banking Crisis.

A lot of people ended up at the bank to get loans against their houses because of many people getting housing mortgages. Then there were more single-family mortgages who in the end failed to pay resulting in an undervaluation of these financial instruments Mortgage-backed securities and credit-default swaps value decreased over time and the market for these ceased to exist. Banks who had offered these financial packages started experiencing a liquidity crisis. Freddie Mac, Fannie Mae, Lehman brother, Royal Bank of Scotland, AIG, HBOS, Merrill Lynch, Alliance &Leicester started filing for bankruptcy. The US federal bank stepped in and started bailing out these banks starting with AIG. Despite government efforts after the crisis, it became very difficult to borrow. Now there were very few people who could get a mortgage and as a result houses prices fell. The collapse of financial institutions was averted by the bailouts, but the stock markets inevitably collapsed. This crisis saw a lot of business closures. Consumer wealth decreases as value slumped in $trillions. All this resulted in the great depression.

The European debt crisis.

Failures of governments of mainly the five coastal countries of Portugal, Spain, Greece, Ireland and Cyprus to bail-out banks requiring assistance from other Eurozone countries, the IMF and the European Central Bank. Most private debts arising from the property were transferred to the countries debt also referred to as the sovereign debt. The use of one currency abated the problem as governments were unable to react faster. The European Financial Stability Facility and the European Stability mechanism were in response to this sovereign debt. The European Central Bank then introduced fiscal measures to combat any further impact. The impact meant the power shift in countries affected and out of the Eurozone in the UK. When the UK financial bubble burst values of securities associated with these fell causing a huge impact on financial institutions. Factors that triggered the financial crisis.

i] Policies to encourage homeownership
ii] easy access to mortgages and credit that later created a bubble and devaluation of financial instruments
iii] Overvaluation of subprime mortgages
iv] flawed trading practices
v] Short term compensation structures
vi] Not enough capital holdings that match the transactions going through.
The Financial Crisis Inquiry Commission concluded that:
"The financial crisis was avoidable and was caused by "widespread failures in financial regulation and supervision", "dramatic failures of corporate governance and risk management at many systemically important financial institutions,``"a combination of excessive borrowing, risky investments and lack of transparency" by financial institutions, ill preparation and inconsistent action by a government that "added to the uncertainty and panic", a "systemic breakdown in accountability and ethics", "collapsing mortgage-lending standards and the mortgage securitization pipeline", deregulation of over-the-counter derivatives, especially credit default swap, and "the failures of credit rating agencies" to correctly price risk." [Wikipedia]

Type 3 Error.

The solution proposed in this case is viable and effective the only problem being that it has been applied to the wrong situation. Otherwise, if the situation was correct, it could have worked. In short, the solution is not for this problem. I think you are asking yourself: what? Yes, this occurs when someone has experienced a similar situation then adopts the methods used for that situation and applies it to a similar but different scenario with the resultant that the method proposed will cause the total collapse of that situation that the people will be in a worse situation than when it was in the first place. The proposed solution and financial stimulus adopted were not correct for the situation. There were fundamental differences that threaten the fabric of the whole system. I will address this issue in detail.

i] 9/11 affected people who were not homeowners in the towers were destroyed. The towers were privately leased and had nothing to do with the government. Although 2996 people died, these people had their houses away from the World Trade Center. Everyone who died at the World Trade Center was at a place of work or enjoying a business meeting of some kind.

Ii] No one, in this case, was made homeless simply because the destroyed building was for commercial and business purposes only.

iii] There was no compensation linked to a loss of house money that can be used or plowed back to the housing market as a deposit. All compensation and insurance were life insurance that had nothing to do with the housing market or acquiring housing.

iv] Lowering and relaxing of regulations aimed at the housing market and the need for people to afford a house were good methods but wrong in this situation because the people who died did not lose their houses where this would be an effective corrective method.

v] Low-interest rates only made it easy to fuel people high mortgage rates without the base input related to the housing market.

vi] The Federal government overrode anti-predatory laws something that encouraged predatory lending with the hope of making a kill.

vii] The government implicitly guaranteed some mortgage lending through Fannie Mae and Freddie Mac.

Solutions for the wrong problem. Third Type Error.

Having said that, I want to argue that all the above issues would be perfect in a different situation. If people's houses were destroyed by the 9/11 attacks, then all the above points would be an idea to initiate a recovery of the economy. The fact that a private complex with commercial and business uses was destroyed surely points to the inadequacies of the fiscal stimulus adopted by the federal reserve and the US government. All the above points would have averted problems in the future but what happened was an intentional fueling of the burst of the housing bubble and the resultant problems. The idea here being that which might be called a hot air situation in that a beautiful situation is created on false grounds that further exacerbate the situation until when the truth comes out then the people realize that the beautiful situation is not that beautiful after all with the result that there is an immediate abandoning of such a thought that it collapses automatically as no one will subscribe to that idea anymore. Those who have invested in such a beautiful idea find themselves with overvalued status that soon evaporates when reality hits home.

The opposite should have been the fiscal policies adopted by the government in order to stimulate the economy, especially considering that 9/11 had nothing to do with the housing market. That raises suspicious to why the government would adopt such fiscal stimulus? At first, you might think that okay this benefited the people. Okay, they did benefit but for a short while as loans from banks pass through the consumer network but the repayments with a contribution to the principal were itself a trigger of future problems. The only reason that makes sense is that the government did this deliberately to financially cripple the people in perpetuation. This is interesting considering that just a day before the 9/11 attacks the government was missing $2,3 trillion. This makes sense only when the government wanted to recover the money from the people. In other words, they adopted and implemented a method called Ball Rolling. Another reason could be that they received bad advice.

9/11 as a deliberate trigger for the collapse of the economy.

The idea here is that of taking money out of the consumer network in trillions.
To understand my arguments, let's look at a case where the adopted corrective and stimulus packages would have been

perfect for that situation. Again, as throughout this report and the first Volume we look at the great fire of London in 1666. This is the best situation for the proposed methods. This is simply because residential houses mainly were destroyed making the proposing solutions perfect for such. In 1666 the fire destroyed people's houses leaving 70 000 people homeless. In this case, the packages to be adopted would focus on providing houses and making mortgagees affordable and easy to get.

A package for such a scenario would be exactly like the points noted above. The people whose houses are destroyed get compensation from insurance companies and loans and mortgages from banks linked to the destroyed houses.

i] The insurance money would be directly associated with the destroyed houses and that means there is a high chance that the money obtained would be plowed back into the housing and mortgage-related market. That cushions the market as some money is obtained back in the market as deposits toward houses. The fact that the 9/11 attacks destroyed commercial and business premises meant those who were getting mortgages had no enough deposit money strictly related to the insurance of housing and loans related to houses.

ii] Any attempt to lax lending regulations and issuing or mortgages would only lead to problems in the future. This is simply because the people are given mortgages they cannot afford to repay. Or mortgages that will have a balloon payment at the end that is way too high to what the people can afford.

iii] In the 9/11 scenario there was no what can be said as the multiplier effect that would have stimulated growth. To explain this let's look at 1666 after the Great Fire of London. 70 000 people were made homeless. Through the courts, the people got compensation and insurance money which they used toward the building of the houses. That would mean more jobs in the housing market as construction companies are brought in to rebuild the houses. The money from insurance or compensation obtained through courts is plowed back into the housing market. These people pay higher deposits toward the building of the houses reducing the mortgage principal and making sure that these lending institutions have capital reserves as well. That would have meant also that only people who could afford (people who got a loan, and a mortgage linked to the destroyed house) the repayment would take mortgages. The government's stance was not to help people but to give them a false sense of security for some time then take even the little money they have that in the end, they would be in a worse off position. In the end, the people would not afford to pay that leads to repossession leaving the people poor without savings and or houses. Even if they hold on to the houses, in the end, they would be left in a worse situation as this will create a balloon payment. The fiscal stimulus adopted by the Federal Reserve would be ideal in a situation of large-scale reconstruction of houses perfect for a situation like after the 1666 Great fire. If the situation is applied to a scenario like 9/11 where not houses of the people were destroyed. The resultant is just a short-term false sense of security before financial disaster strikes.

Ball rolling and A False Sense of Security.

I argued that this only makes sense if, for example, the idea is to pass the missing $2,3 trillion to the people; the consumers. In that case, all the fiscal stimulus adopted was to take money out of the economy and from the consumers as well. Simply the government passing its debt to the economy. Picture a man throwing a small-money-collecting-ball that attracts money that is in the economy. That ball rolls down the economy collecting every money in the economy at the same time becoming bigger and bigger as it rolls until it's too heavy that it sinks down through the government mine shaft until it rolls back to the government to the man who rolled it in the first place. The idea is to provide high value at first that people use their savings aiming at making even more within a short period. They spend the little they have on overvalued houses just because the government has lowered interest rates and that the mortgage is simply affordable and easily available. The little people have saved is used as a deposit for the houses.

The more people find it easy to get loans for houses the lower houses prices in the long run. People, in the end, have high mortgages and overvalued but low house values. That causes then to refinance again and again as prices continuous fall. In the end, the people's hopes are dashed they not only lose the houses due to foreclosures, but they would have lost their savings too.

9/11 as a deliberate event to cause the financial collapse of the economy.

In this case, I will argue that 9/11 was a pre-planned event by someone very intelligent and someone who knows about past events like the Great Fire of London of 1666 and or other fire and different economic situations. It's like poisoning a system knowingly that in the end, the situation will collapse. In this sense, 9/11 is used as a cover of the real intent of creating a situation like that. That brings me to the other point. Who would gain much given the current circumstances? First, let's analyze the consequences.

Consequences.

There are investment companies out there that have been there for centuries that pool their resources together in syndicates and so on that rely on even the smallest increase in certain financial instruments and commodities. All these resulted in a drop in stock markets. The idea behind the stock markets is for companies to raise money through buying and selling of shares. The idea is that companies and investors can only make real serious money if a crash happens. Therefore, if you were in the business of investing in stocks, you will be aiming for a crash to make it big. Given that for some this can be a billion dollars invested with institutions like the Lloyd's Market where it is a regulating body that coordinates syndicates with values in $billions.

Why do stock market crash?

Mainly due to certain economic factors and people's behavior. Panic and loss of confidence by investment banks and companies can cause the stock market to crash too. In most cases, a sharp stock share fall signals the end of an economic bubble. This is an inflated value of an asset that simply deflates because people realize that it's not as valued as it is labeled. That causes everyone dealing with these assets to devalue those assets and start counting losses. A method called Debt deflation.

Debt Deflation.

This is a situation that can be induced and manipulated by someone who wanted to see a recession and its consequence of stock fall. The idea is to do reverse engineering to induce conditions that will lead to a recession. The idea is to create a situation where people would end up defaulting on their consumer loans and mortgages. Bank assets would fall in value as more and more people default. As people default the banks would write off the value of debt thereby reducing the value. The default, in this case, is larger than money set aside to cushion such defaults. This leads to a spike in bank insolvencies. The banks then tighten the lending and spending shrinks too.

Intentional Inducing the Debt Deflation.

The idea in this report is that debt deflation is manipulated by people investing in stock to cause future drastic stock fall so that they can make a lot of money. This is simply just like in the 9/11 attacks. The attacks are used to make people feel vulnerable; human nature when you watch something destroyed as such the general sense is to find strong long-term accommodation. It a physiological manipulation tool that is easily used to humans to induce certain conditions. Let's look at the Great Fire of London in 1666. Watching that huge fire engulfing houses would leave people insecure and the very thing that would come to mind is protection. A strong house and someone who can defend them against that fire. Looking at 9/11 this is too the same. The idea is to induce a sense of insecurity. If people have witnessed the destruction of the 'perceived strongest and tallest buildings' fear would make them put security as a priority for at least two years until the impacts of the events starts wearing off. The first two years after such an event people would have that event so clear in their minds that they tend to choose policies they would not have gone for if the event had not happened. Providing incentives to buy houses after the event people would want to buy strong and secure houses of their own instead of renting. We see the same tactics being used here. At first, the fiscal stimulus seems to have the people in mind. Housing for all. Elimination of anti-predatory tactics. Encouraging Fannie Mae and Freddie Mac to provide ways in which the low-and middle-income households can access mortgages. The Federal Reserve's lowering of interest rates all have the effect of making getting a mortgage attractive. After people's securities have been exposed then fiscal policies and economic stimulants play another role in helping the insecure people to purchase houses in the belief to make them have a sense of security real or perceived. The people use their savings to pay for deposits of houses. Most people on rented or leased accommodation because of the event would tend to switch to secure owned housing. The favorable conditions at that time make people make haste unrealistic decisions. The low-interest rates make everything look affordable. For the two years following the event, the people spend on 'defense' housing themselves. Money that would otherwise be spent on other things would be spent on housing. The government as well will match the consumers and spend more on defense but in the form of military. The more the people get mortgages and borrow loans from banks the more the prices rise until such a time when it's hard to get the loan. More people start defaulting as they have used their savings as deposits for the house. This time is characterized by inflated prices and values until when the bubble bursts. Then banks and mortgage lenders would stop lending.

Prices fall. Houses are repossessed. Foreclosure and mortgage refinancing characterize this period. In the end, people default on loan and mortgage repayment. Bank assets decrease in value. In the end, the banks crash as well, in the end, you have a self-induced debt deflation and a recession. Stock market and stock prices go to the highest just before the collapse.

9/11 As a Prediction Tool.

I am here going to look at the Lloyd Stock Market not because it is involved or what not simply because it operates in a way different from most investment markets in that it is a corporate body that acts as a regulator. It brings people together, the buyers and sellers who then form a syndicate. These syndicate's role is to pool and spread risk not literally though although it's something relevant here. The members of the syndicate are known as the underwriters or Names who are corporations, investment banks, and individuals. The interesting thing with this market is that it based on marine insurance. In 2017 the syndicate total asset value amounted to more than $50 billion dollars, with more than $25 billion of members assets. More than $3billions of the money belonged to third links. [Wikipedia]. Interesting to note here which is not confined to Lloyd's Market just using this as an example is the Sasse scandal described above. In short, there was a case of inflating the value of property in Newyork South Bronx and then maliciously ensure the properties at a very high value. Shortly after that, the property suffers an arson attack that automatically makes the owner of the insurance a millionaire in this case in the tune of $40 million. We know that 9/11 can be regarded as a similar case assuming that the attacks were deliberate. We see that shortly after insuring the World Trade Center towers ended up in smoke in this case not regarding how they were brought down. We see him getting $4,55 billion for the towers as insurance. My point here is not to arrive at conclusions this way. All in this report from Volume I, I am looking at known facts and then arrive at the conclusion. I have done everything possible to avoid falling into the reverse engineering trap. I am applying what I described as the role of precedence to arrive at conclusion. Having said that, we know that stock markets, especially like Lloyd's Market, are based on what is called Marine insurance. These markets bring together syndicates that deal with insurances. Their job here is to pool and spread risks. The idea here is that if you are selling the insurance, you make money if nothing happens to the people who have bought the insurance. Straight forward. Let us say you insure a house in the tropics and no hurricane or floods damages your house your premiums won't go high and the insurance provider will not spend money. Come to a hurricane then something must give. This Lloyd's Market suffered a loss of $50 million as hurricane Betsy struck. This is because when they're no hurricane or other calamities the market benefited as it collects all this money. Okay, let's look at marine insurance.

Marine Insurance.

This covers any damage to ships, cargo, terminals or any transport. Marine Insurance is often combined with Aviation and Transit (cargo) risks and is known as MAT.
"A marine policy typically covered only three-quarters of the insured's liabilities towards third parties (Institute Time Clauses Hulls 1.10.83)."
[Wikipedia]. Liabilities arose due to three things.
i] Collisions between ships.
ii] Collision with a fixed object an Allison
iii] Wreck removal
Since the other quarter was not covered by the insurance company the shipowners themselves grouped to form bands in order to ensure and cover the remaining quarter themselves. This led to the Protection and Indemnity Clubs.

Use of A cycloid As A Prediction Tool.

A cycloid can be drawn to show which points will correspond to the points that can be drawn as points of impact on the world trade center. A cycloid was used to show a projection 10 years to the future to show how things are going to be from 2001. I explained above under our actors namely Christopher Wren. We know he was interested in mathematics, astronomy, architecture, and physic among other things. He spent time at the Royal Society carrying out experiments and meeting and talking with a leading physicist like Isaac Newton. He wrote a paper on cycloid that was published answering a question that was asked. He realized that a circle can move in one direction without slipping and thereby forming a curve over time. In other words, if given the initial parameters a projectile curve can be constructed. A circle can be drawn and be divided in accordance with a clock. Twelve parts from I to 12. A horizontal line is drawn and marked in matching equal parts from 0 to twelve. Assume the circle is spinning and a 1 on the circle touches the horizontal line at point 1 too and so on. Draw another horizontal line in the middle of a circle parallel to the x-axis. Join the linking point 1 with 1, 2 with 2, etc. and then draw a curve joining all the points. The cycloid equation is:

$x = r (\theta - \sin \theta)$

and $y = r (1 - \cos \theta)$.

For a single hump of the cycloid arc length is 8a where a is a constant and area is;

$A = 3\pi A$

In stock dealing the cycloid will show the stock market curve in years from the time of the event. This was used in line with other parameters like the Timeball value which was depicted by the time WTC7 took to fall. We know the WTC7 fell in 6,6 seconds. The value is always in years. So, to be precise those equipped with this idea would know that the maximum points or the highest value of the shares before the curve or price start to fall is determined by this value. The graph will show the highest points on the curve. This point can be the highest the stock value will attain before falling. This will be a time that will signal a sell. People will make the highest returns if the sale at that time. After that, the prices will fall rapidly before the market crashes. When this happens, it would be ideal also to buy as you will be buying low and hope to sell high. The cycloid will give you a guideline to exact time frames this will happen. A syndicate would benefit the most because the investment money poured into the stock markets is large and the returns tend to be large also even though the money is divided among several players. The above equation will indicate the position reached as the highest point before the curve starts dipping. θ will be the angle in degrees. For example, the angle of impact by the plane that hits the North tower was 45 degrees from true North position whereas the plane that impacted the south tower impacted it at 340 degrees from North in a clockwise direction. This could explain why the plane made nearly turned in a circle before impacting the tower. These were coordinates. Y is the vertical axis of the graph and x is the horizontal axis. Then if we have the coordinates obtained will show the points on the graph where the y-axis meets the x-axis. We know that r is the radius of the circle we have drawn. We know π is a mathematical constant value that can be substituted. It is =3.14159. Calculating will give us the coordinates of the highest point on the graph. At this point, it's a sell signal because the price or value will not exceed this point. It is the maximum point the highest point the shares' value will reach before they start to fall.

$x = r (\theta - \sin \theta)$

and $y = r (1 - \cos \theta)$.

Circumference is pi (π) times the diameter. c= πd

Radius (r) = diameter divided by 2= d/2

We know that a cycloid is half of a circle.

We know half of the cycloid hump as 8a where a is a constant.

C/2= πd/2

8a/2=3.14159xd/2

4a=2r x1,57

4a=πr

4a=3.14159r

r=1.17a

sin 45∘=1√2

45∘ as a fraction =45/360=0.125

x = r (45° - sin 45)

x=1.17a (45°-sin45)

x=1.17a (45°-0.707)

x=1.17a (0.125-0.707)

x=1.17a (-0.58 2)

x=0.68a

A is a constant that is normally given a value of 9,9999999 or simply 10

Then x becomes 0.68x 10

x=0.68x10

x=6.8 that is 6 years eight months.

On the axis of the graph, the highest point will be 6 years and 8 months from the day of the event. This value will give us time on the axis of the graph. So, we know it will take at least 6 years and 8 months from the day of the attacks to the highest point the stock prices will reach.

Attacks happened in 2001 in September which we can write as 2001,9 plus 6.8

x= 2008.7

We now know that the highest point the shares would reach their highest value will be before 6 years and 8 months from the day of the impact that is 2001 September (2001.9).

We know that x is 2008.7

We are sure that roughly the highest point before shares start to fall is before July 2008. After that, it will be a crash.

We don't look at the y-axis because we want to know the time and date this will happen. Y-axis will give us the value. We don't worry about the value, so I am not going to calculate the value of y. We want to know when this will happen. So, the axis of a graph is used for time. We are sure we know somewhere before 2008 in July the highest point will be reached before the crash occurs. This is time to sell and wait for the complete collapse then after that

buy low again.
See the image of George W Bush in the school at the elementary school on the day of the attacks.
Check this link.
   https://upload.wikimedia.org/wikipedia/commons/0/02/George_W._Bush_with_burning_towers_on_television.jpg

CHAPTER SIX

There was a call for a stand down. They let it happen.
Rules of Engagement as a reason for the stand down.

This was the reason cited in the 12 October 2000 USS Cole attack by the same group that carried out the 9/11 attacks. A small boat approached with civilians and the navy officers in the ship did not react even after 17 sailors were killed. They were afraid to be court-martialed if they retaliate when a second small boat appeared. It is not clear cut and certain procedures have to be followed even though the captain must take every reasonable step to avoid or reduce casualties. This can be said to be true also given that the planes were carrying US citizens it would require possibly the President and Congress's authorization to target an airplane carrying hundreds of America citizens. I think the terrorist had a hostage situation in mind. They were sure they can carry out the attacks without being stopped as it was like a hostage situation where rules of engagement had to be followed. It's not a clear-cut option. They could simply have delayed knowing that it would be worse if they acted. Killing four terrorists, as well as hundred Americans, probably would be hard to justify if court-martialed. I think the terrorists knew they can get away with this. Also, assuming it was a surprise attack they were caught off guard even NORAD the North American Aerospace Defense had no chance. It all happened so fast and above all the hijackers disconnected the transponders or switched coordinates. Even though they have deterred, detect and defend moto they had no chance. Too late to react. Jets could be scrambled fast.

I first argued in Volume I that the government after the announcement that it was losing money with $2,3 trillion missing, they decided that enough was enough. The system they were using was obsolete. I went further to explain that centuries back on 11 September 1853 a miracle happened. There was the first use of the electric telegraph that rendered the Telegraph Hill and the Point Lobos obsolete. These communication hills were based on a primitive way of communication called the semaphore system. A semaphore structure was used to pass information to the people about the kind of ship entering the harbor and what kind of goods it was carrying. This method replaced man and horse. This method made the hills very popular and often people would gather as the ship approached the harbor. Those days information was money and traders, speculators, buyers and dealers all required this information. Advanced technology in the form of electric telegraph rendered this method obsolete together with the Telegraph Hill and the Point Lobos. Do you know that the Twin Towers idea was based on these communication hills? The inner hill was used to gather with the outer hill that acted as the lookout point that would convey a message to the inner hill about the kind of ship and the goods it was carrying. People on the outer hill would arrange the semaphore tower with metal blades that were arranged in a certain way to convey the message. The inner hill would then look through a telescope the signing of the blades and interpret the message. After the new way of communication that was faster and reliable, the hills became obsolete. In 2000 the technological advancement had already happened with the rise of the computer age. The paper era had come to an end. Everything had to be computerized. The old system was based on insider trading and this was a bad practice as this meant that some people were exploiting loopholes and making real money at the expense of the government. The problem here is that you can't just change the system from paper to a computer because this will mean a lot of time converting paper into digital. That costs money and time as well. We know that a crash is the only factor that can justify an instant change in the current system. Destroying transaction records is prohibited by federal laws. A new system that is computer-based can be fully implemented only when a crash has brought everything to a standstill without worrying about a lot of stuff. Okay if the idea was to change the system and avoid losing more money on top of the $2,3 trillion already missing then surely the President or any high officials would not stop anyone if this was outsourced. That is one of the reasons that can explain arguments of a stand down.

My second hypothesis is that the President was being blackmailed and as such could not call for a stand-down or avert the attacks. In this hypothesis someone very clever and in this case a foreign nation or let's just call this nation the Beasts II has stolen the missing $2,3 trillion. Their goal to reduce America to its knees so that it accepts protection thereby becoming its protectorate. Their aim is to show America that it needs its protection. Surely $2,3 trillion is serious money to take for granted. The deal here is that the Beast II becomes responsible for America's external threats and the only threat that gives grounds for this is terrorism. America would remain sovereign; all internal affairs are the responsibility of America but when it comes to external international threats of which terrorism is the main one, then it's this Beasts II business. In return, America must agree to go to war side by side with this Beasts II. America has openly declared itself as the most powerful, but this new Superpower is there to prove otherwise. To Beasts II, there can never be another Superpower of the world. After stealing the money and bringing George W Bush face to face with his Nadir; the lowest point of his career this Beast II knows that it has a hand on negotiating a deal. Donald Rumsfeld publicly declared that this man is not in control of his administration. How can he lose $2,3 trillion and do nothing? Maybe he should go. What do you say, George? George cornered has no option because he is guilty, no; but he has no option he can't prove otherwise. Beasts II then tells him what he can do to retain his power and glory. The next day he goes to his best followers who listen no matter what. The only people whom he can talk to without them questioning his authority. The kids at an elementary school. Do this and this as a reality check and see for yourself if anyone follows you or listens to you declared the Beasts II. George is so sure everyone wants him in power and follows him made a bet with the Beast II. Get just 5 followers and you are as free as the wind blowing everywhere it wants and fails to get five then that means you need my protection. You do what I want to help you solve this external threat from international terrorists. Above all whenever we go to war side by side you will get a share of the loot too. We will just say World War II debt even though even then the money your former Presidents gave me was protection fee-money and not a loan. Read between the lines George. Shocked and saddened by the fact that out of the 3000 people likely to die that day only 4 escaped with their lives staying away from the towers George was cornered and trapped as 2996 died. He had no choice but to accept being a secret protectorate of the Beast II. George cursed and looked at the Beasts II.

[Fictional conversation]
"I thought I could be as good as my father."
The Beast II laughed.
"I have heard that before. King Solomon facing rejection and low approval rates as he thought he could be like his Father. Jesus facing rejection and death thinking that he can be easily accepted like his father God. I have seen King Charles II facing the same situation, thinking that he can be easily accepted just because he is a king. King or President without my protection you are nothing. Do as I say, and I will make everyone listen and follow you. In fact, I will make your approval rates the best. All I ask is strength on your part and courage to understand that some have to die for you to gain immortality as the President."
"What do you mean you are going to kill again?"
"We need to persuade people to go to war. Don't worry this time it will be the other external force; from space. We have to "break

Nasser", sorry I mean break NSA."

"No. I cannot do that. The space program set us up there as the only true Superpower without NSA we are nothing."

"A taste of your own medicine some might say. Do you know how fast it took for the WTC2 to collapse to the ground?"

"How am I supposed to know that? You think that when my boys are dying in there, I spend time checking all these trivial things?"

"Trivial? Just like Eisenhower. You don't understand in fact you never understood me. I will tell you. It took 56 minutes to collapse. Does that ring any bells?"

George did not answer he looked puzzled and confused.

"1956! Yes. I know you forgot already, but I did not. I was the Superpower then but you, no. You wanted my glory too."

"Me?"

"It doesn't matter who exactly you represent all. That Eisenhower humiliating me like that costing me the equivalent of $2,3 trillion in today's money. Destroying my plan to break Nasser. But you are going to do what I want. You will go to war as my ally. I will get the oil don't worry you will get your share of the loot. In return, I will eliminate your external threats in the form of terrorists and space threats."

"I can't break NSA."

"You still want to sacrifice more people. Surely don't tempt me."

"That's the worst case of blackmail. You can't get away with this."

"Blackmail? Oh, I see. I will simply put a black male in your place, case solved."

"What? First black male, I mean black President?"

George remained silent after that.

"Why do you look like you have seen a ghost? Can't swallow the idea of a black President? You accused me of blackmail act but what you don't know is that my protection is the ultimate. You say blackmail. I provide a black male. So?"

"I am not bothered black male or white male in the White House. I just wanted to be as good as my father. I am not just a daddy's boy you know?"

"Then do what I am telling you. I can make your dreams come

true."
"Just like my father?"
"You can never be as good as your father. You need protection; my protection. No one can ever be like your father accept that and move on."
"But..."

George looked everywhere looking for the Beast II, but he had already gone. He could hear his horns from far away.
"Black male? Is it that Obama guy?"
[End of fictional scenario]
The New World Order Fulfilling the Prophecy.
The third hypotheses why the government might have called for a stand down and allowed the attacks to happen is the fact that whatever was happening was beyond mankind. It was something beyond the realm of humanity. The prophecy was being fulfilled. The idea behind this is the idea I advanced at the beginning of this report and in Volume I. First you might not believe in the bible but for argument's sake just pretend you do in the end it will make sense. To recap. People believed that there must be a God so powerful that he created earth and us. God set rules for a man to follow to give mankind his "Protection". But mankind broke the rules knowing that God was unjustly forbidding him to see the light and live like gods above all and open the door to longevity. Meaning living forever. In Genesis 3v22 God admitted that mankind had eaten the fruits and gained the wisdom to know what is good and what is evil. Mankind has become like God. In Revelations 13v 1-18 mind you these are future prophecy written and sealed to be witnessed in the future. Modern-day people take advantage of these scriptures and interpret them now. Some have gone to lengths to make sure the prophecies are fulfilled. So, if you don't believe in God here is your justification for that. We see in Genesis 3v22 era it was acknowledged that some humans have gained extraordinary knowledge and power to the standards of God. But because mankind is made of flesh, he will experience a lot of pain if he is to do God's job. Simply because God kills people

to balance nature through earthquakes, floods, etc. Now we see some people who makes no sense of all this. Simply because they can't understand why if God is good why he is associated with death and suffering faced by man? Revelations tries to answer that. Some people have become like God and are in the form of the Beast I and Beast II in Revelations 13v1-18. God just to prove a point has let these beats take over but not forever but just for 24 months. He made a bet that pain and fear would make a man surrender trying to be God and take his correct place as one under God and under his protection. As a protectorate. This creates the idea of the New World Order. There shall come an era when man will be like God and everything he does is in the name of God. God has delegated his role to these beasts.

Revelation 13 King James Version (KJV)

13 And I stood upon the sand of the sea, and saw a beast rise out of the sea, having seven heads and ten horns, and upon his horns ten crowns, and upon his heads the name of blasphemy.
...
5 And there was given unto him a mouth speaking great things and blasphemies, and power was given unto him to continue forty and two months.
6 And he opened his mouth in blasphemy against God, to blaspheme his name, and his tabernacle, and them that dwell in heaven.
7 And it was given unto him to make war with the saints, and to overcome them: and power was given him over all kindreds, and tongues, and nations.
8 And all that dwell upon the earth shall worship him, whose names are not written in the book of life of the Lamb slain from the foundation of the world.
9 If any man has an ear, let him hear.

10 He that leadeth into captivity shall go into captivity: he that killeth with the sword must be killed with the sword. Here is the

patience and faith of the saints.

Now we see the beasts working day and night, especially the second beast who applies to this situation. The second Beasts is a devious and manipulating beast doing whatever it takes to

i] mark everyone on earth, rich or poor, presidents or buggers, intellectuals or laymen all shall be tagged given a mark on the forehead or right hand or a serial number. They shall join a cult, a New World Order. Participation shall be permitted only if they can show the marks as proof of belonging to the cult. All this costs a lot of money. All technological advances are prophesied and foretold in the bible. Of interest here is the need for tagging or creating serial numbers and software that can help to achieve that including storage and recording devices. Each person shall be given a small personal computer. All these cost money. Therefore, all that is happening is for the benefit of the cult of the New World Order. This Beast II is in God's shoes and has God's approval to try to do his job that involves killing to balance nature. The only drawback is that man or the Beast II has no powers like God to cause an earthquake or a flood so how can he kill? In Revelation, it is written that he will deceive and manipulate. We see now he is taking advantage of the people tricking them. So, people believe this is part of the big plan. Whatever is happening is part of the bigger picture. To tag and give marks to everyone on earth, the Beast II has several options.

i] On birth. The easiest trick in the bible dating back to the days of King Herod who authorized midwives to tag newborn babies of foreigners at birth as population control and to preserve his kingdom.

ii] The foreigners were not born in this country, so chances are that they are not marked on birth. This is the main reason. To enable and place measures to do this first before our people die. That justifies like the experiments of a one Christopher Wren discussed above who created a transparent enclosure like Guantanamo Bay to soften the opposition and give all foreigners not born here the 'English Honey', a Mark of the Beast II as in Revelations to easily control them. The men are taken away from their wives and the wives are given new men with a better social standing. They start breeding and to the world, this should appear as perfect an ideal world with no race divisions but deep down the children born from this setting will have the status of their mother and not their father assuming all fathers be white and the mother's ethnic. People will assume the children are free with social standing as their fathers but in reality, they have the status of their mothers. Why? So as to justify marking them with marks on foreheads and right hand or tagging them giving them serial numbers. All this must be done to fulfill the prophecy. Money from the oil proceeds will be used for massive technological advancement to fulfill all the prophecies. Therefore, what is happening can't be stopped. Its above humanity. This is a preparation of a New World Order. It is a divine calling.

The fourth hypothesis why the government called for a stand-down is in two parts. First to justify and signal the need to go to war. Secondly as Fraud efficiency. I covered in detail the 1960 Eisenhower and the Anglo-French Suez Canal incident. Eisenhower refused to go to war as an ally of the Anglo-French simply because the canal was a trivial matter to him. He had better things to do than waste time fighting the Egyptians for the canal. In reply he declared that he did not see the Suez Canal as that important as the nationalization of the canal was not like nationalization of oil wells [which] depletes a country's resources. Now we see Donald Rumsfeld announcing that $2,3 trillion has been paid for oil and oil-related products like jet fuel. Something they saw as a waste of resources when all they can do is go to war (Mind you Rumsfeld is the Secretary of Defense at the time of the announcement) and make this oil a common good for the enjoyment of everyone. So, in this case, the money is not missing but has been used to buy oil and related products. The Pentagon has paid this money to foreigners for oil resources, but the good news is that it is recoverable. How and why Donald Rumsfeld said that? They can simply go to war and recover the cost and save or reduce any future costs. To show the people that war is not just necessary but is a must if we are to balance our books. The second reason is to cover inefficiency in what I called fraud efficiency. Destroying paper records such a way will cause massive structural damage to financial records. It's like hiding the evidence to cover any fraudulent activities. I have covered this topic above. What happened was to create a situation like 9/11 when people are given a sense of insecure and vulnerable that they end up looking for security that they end up being closer to the President. Those who rent flats and lease from private landlords will be discouraged to do that instead the people would look for their own accommodation in the form of houses. The government then makes the offer of an own house irresistible. Low-interest rates and other factors all make it easy to get mortgages, especially from the young and single-family. This takes all the savings and channel money towards repaying the mortgages and the loans. This is the third type of error. They provided solutions to the wrong problem. In the end, all money is taken from the consumers and the economy back to the government. The people default on loans and mortgages. Banks restrict lending. The economy shrinks, then there are job cuts, then a recession, the stock prices fall. This is can be said to have been deliberately induced to correct the initial missing of the whopping $2,3 trillion from the government. A reversal effect takes back money from the economy and the consumers into government coffers. Here we end up with all banks now begging the government for help to bail them out of bankruptcy and insolvency.

Lastly as a Power Ball.

This can be proof of a protection argument. This can be seen as a power game the best script for a movie if you like. At first, we have a weak President based and judged by many as being a daddy's boy. He is one of the presidents to go to the office with fewer votes. He soon becomes unpopular with low approval rates. One regarded as a cowboy who has no clue to the advanced dealings of the Pentagon. I can only assume that most government members maybe were plotting against him trying to

bring him down. He might have sensed that they wanted to do him a-Jesus. Assuming the second Beast II came to his rescue then the events were just to make the people respect him. You might say a manual of how to rebuild a "Nadir to a Zenith" in other words how to pick one at the lowest point in his career to elevate him to the highest levels. A form of protection if you like. The question here is that; Is he prepared to go through with the plan even if it means heartbreak and sadness? If yes, then we see the manipulation and deception of the Beast II. We see the use of tricks. Provision of solutions to a wrong problem. What is happening is a ball rolling strategy? Shifting of blame if you like. Initially, the White House is to blame. But Bush (fictional) declared that it was his fault he has been misled, given the wrong information if you like. But the people are adamant that it's his fault. He realized that in order to believe him they must go through what he went through. The Beast II then shouted. "Leave that to me."
We have reversal policies employed in the end. We have people now crying that their money is 'missing'. We have banks crying for help from the President. All people crying to the President; "Saves us! Save us." The mighty banks now beg the President for help and to bail them out. A true heroic ending. The President from his lowest point (the Nadir) to his highest point the Zenith. A true hero ending. Protection justified by the presence of hostile external threats of which terrorism is the major one. Hence also the rise and growth of external terrorism justifies the existence of such protection. No terrorists no this kind of protection. Power versus collateral damage?

Food for thought.

Is there a chance that people would entice terrorists acts for $2,3 trillion? To justify going to war to get oil and save government oil product's expenditure bill? What is the role of a 10-year-War Contingency-Plan in all this? A topic covered in Volume I. A very good example being the fact that in 1949 a 10-year-war-contingency plan was in place even before the events of 1960 happened. In that case are all these acts means to an end (the war goals) or ends in themselves? We know too that the President of the USA Eisenhower requested that secret bases for planes be established in Pakistan in order to spy on the Soviet Union. We know too he outsourced his activities of spying using the British Royal Navy. We know too he sent his own men to spy on the Soviet Union resulting in the 1960 U2 incident. We found him in the same shoes as Bush's being accused of not in control of his administration. A one Cannon decided to stir his end by addressing the House of Representatives himself something the President was supposed to do and spilling the beans. The President faced with a risk of losing his job by admitting that he sent the pilot to spy, an act regarded as an act of aggression. He admitted to such an unconventional behavior but highlighted that the threat of Weapons of Mass Destruction outweighed anything. He cited Pearl Harbor and declared that the threat of surprise attacks was real and needed attention. That saved his job. Years later we see George W Bush taking responsibility for wanting to go to war but not admitting to any involvement in the terrorist acts. Just like Eisenhower the real threat are Weapons of Mass Destruction. I can only assume that George W Bush adopted a stance done by a one Gamal Abdel Nasser of Egypt in 1956 giving a direct command concealed as a speech. We know from Volume I of this book that Nasser mentioned the French dam builder 13 times giving a command to take the canal at that time and nationalizing it. I think George W Bush did a Nasser too. When he said; "our freedoms have been attacked," I think he was telling those in government to do that because what followed can only be described as the "attack of our freedoms". The main thing is the WMDs. They did not find any WMDs. That brings me to my next question. Why WMDs?

CHAPTER SEVEN

Weapons of Mass Destruction.

God has given some people on earth wisdom to such an extent that they now understand what is good and evil. Understand the dealings of nature and how the world operates. These people have eaten the fruits of life and can act like gods. They are like God himself. The only thing they lacked is the power to use nature to cause death and destruction like what God does. If humanity knew really what this means surely the world would be not like it is today. People of today are blinded by earthly things. If some people are in the process of creating Weapons of Mass Destruction in your face are you not supposed to be afraid? If a lion you have never seen in real life, but you heard before that it kills and eats humans is approaching you are you not supposed to be afraid and run away? I used to think that it is human nature that if there are dangerous people run away? If someone is playing God making WMDs themselves surely humanity should be scared. God himself was scared that if mankind is given wisdom, he will use that wisdom to try to sidestep him and in doing so will kill his people just to prove that he can be God and God's replacement. Such a person is not God but the Beast I, and the Beast II and the Dragon setting fires everywhere as per commands of the Beasts I. This is what is happening in real life. It doesn't matter whether you believe there is a God or not. This is happening. The question is are you sure you are going to be part of a third of the population that will be saved not by God but by these beasts playing God. Believe it or not, the bible is like a manual of how to do things. There are things written there that haven't happened but things that will drive mankind to extremes in order to fulfill these prophecies. It does not matter that you don't read the bible or believe in God. Earthly people have assumed the role of a god. Just like you these people are so educated and advanced like you that they don't believe a God exists. Even if he exists, he is not on earth what is on earth is the responsibility of mankind to try to balance nature. Common sense the more people live on earth the more pressure is put on resources and infrastructure the more the people will fight wars. It is a fact that for the past 2000 years mankind was acting as God hiding behind religion, the bible and the Quran but himself correcting the needed balance through wars. Imagine if there were no wars at all and how many people would have lived on earth at one time? Man, today is God. If you don't believe in God at least this makes sense to you. Common sense has prevailed over centuries. Our fast thinkers who are our forefathers have written the bible to give us a manual on how to live forever to preserve humanity without extinction. Whether you believe there is a God or not makes no difference. I have never seen God one might say but everyone has seen a man. As the population grows and improvement in technology and medicine increases as well less and fewer people die which is good. That's the idea of life. It makes sense also that this should be something everyone aspires to do. But in reality, it is just a dream. Mankind is unable to priorities his goals in line with the growing population.

The ideal world.

In what I call the ideal world we will have people living longer as technology advance as well. Fewer and fewer people die everyone aims to preserve life and bring the best out in people. People are great thinkers and they don't stop thinking about ways to improve life and accommodate the growing population. All resources are channeled back with the aim of finding better ways of doing things, better energy sources, better ways of accommodating everyone, elimination of boundaries, etc. In this world it's a perfect system there are no third type errors. Life is simply problem A is solved by problem B. Everyone works together as a whole and have one goal: for the betterment of humanity. But such a system today can't be achieved because mankind's brain is still in the defensive era. We lived for 2000 years yet mankind still acts the same way as the first man centuries ago. His main fear was the fear of surprise attacks. Okay, then I understand. There were all kinds of creatures. Dinosaurs and probably aliens too but trust me after 2000 years I can tell you all that all surprise attacks are from mankind himself. We as a people have not developed at all. Our brain is still in the early years thinking about war and defense. All the resources that would be used for the betterment of mankind as in the ideal world above are used to make the most destructive weapons. $trillions worldwide is spent on weapons money that could be used for the ideal world. Who are our enemies? Are there aliens to visit us? We had reached a turning point once of moving away from defensive economies to superior advanced stages where cooperation and networking are paramount than defense. But man, as a man, he wants to stick to what he knows best; defensive economies based on weapons and wars and segregation and boundaries that keep on feeding wars after wars. The idea behind this is that there is no God we are our own gods. It is us as mankind to maintain the balance in nature through wars. Some people I think in the 1960s realized that man can live happily without wars or weapons as nature intended or as God intended depending on your beliefs. All we need to do is put our priorities right. Let's move away from these defensive economies. Year after year we are spending $trillions on defense all this money can be used to find ways of making food, new energy sources, find new accommodation in other planets so earth sustains the growing populadion. Then some politicians afraid to take the challenge started talking about aliens. Back to defensive economies again. More and more money on weapons. The vicious circle is repeated and again. Resources that could be used somewhere else ends up being used to make the greatest

weapons.
I ask you a question.
"If everyone in the world somehow was your brother or your sister and you had just won the USA PowerBall and for argument's sake you now have $trillion. Would you embark on making the best weapons? (Assuming there are no threats of aliens at all which is true).
If your answer is no, then what would you do?
Obvious common sense; to make a better life for everyone.
No! Hold! You Communist again?
It's not socialist views but a better understanding of the role of mankind on earth. If you today (in your mind) remove all boundaries and become blind to all our differences and you have just won, the USA Megamillions is a weapon on your list for things to do for that year? If the answer is no, then there is something wrong with us. The bible Revelations was written a long time ago 2000 years ago, yet it has things that haven't happened yet. Let's say people at the beginning sat down and analyzed the world and proposed solutions to all potential issues mankind would face in the future and what they came up with is a manual of acted problems with solutions collected in the form of the bible. If you believe in God, then still that does not change anything. These people realized that mankind, in the end, would be stupid like today. He will do his best to eradicate diseases and provide excellent living styles as nature intended but will keep making weapons and use the war as a nature-balancing-tool. In this case, mankind must be defensive and keep spending all resources on weapons. These people sat down again and decided that if that kept going on a New World Order was needed to avert the extinction of mankind.

The New World Order.

This is the new solution to mankind and the only way that will make mankind move away from defensive economies to superior economies that encourage networking and cooperation. Mankind after this will stop to be bothered about defense and weapons. These people after 2000 years have realized that they are their own worst enemies and as such there was no need to keep making weapons. They have such an understanding that they realized that the purpose of mankind is to do whatever it takes to better human life. Admire beauty does whatever it takes to enjoy the best things in life. We must play God by doing better than God. Looking for better ways of improving life. No men in this world will even think of doing harm to another man or think of making digital agents that imitate diseases. No man shall let another man play God everyone will be clever to know, and they will not need the protection of the Beasts. People will spend money not on weapons but on other things linking the whole world as one. That requires a lot of money and no one shall even think of making weapons. For who? Everyone will be your brother or sister. Mankind will have evolved and would have become like God. This stage is what most people synonymous with heaven but if there is no God then this must happen here on earth one day. Mankind is still not grasping this that most think that there is another stage probably in heaven. But no. This is a stage that will happen here on earth. It should have happened already, but we are fearful and to be honest, can't be asked to give up what we all think as important for our security; stupid weapons. Mankind has been stubborn. He can't change year after year we watch him doing the same thing quarreling, manipulating, fighting and all kinds of evil. Still spending the scare resources on the mightiest weapons when others are suffering yet they have been there stealing resources and all the like. Just like the arguments advanced in Volume I change can only come after a crash. An event so horrific that mankind will dig holes underneath and ask the earth to bury them alive. A crash of some kind will inevitably make mankind realize that there are more important things to life than just a war. If his main concern is balancing nature, then that will be looked at in the future. A crash now will remove that need to keep checking and balancing nature. A plan is already in place and as we speak it is in the development stages. The beasts as in

Revelations 13 v1-18 are at work right now.

The roles of the Beasts in Revelations 13v 1-18.

The beasts are there to cause a crash so bad that people will think it is the end of the day. Mankind is his nature not to change unless something bad has happened, but don't you worry, we have the Beasts to take care of that. These Beasts are humans and not gods. They are just like you among others. They will act as agents approved by God that is if you believe in God. If not, then they are chosen by the few people at the beginning who sat down and decided to write manuals to guide mankind to avoid the extinction of mankind. These people realized that some people will be needed to act as God to kill to balance nature and above all to destroy all people of these generations with stupid genes that they insist on defensive economies. The few who are to remain shall be wise enough like Gods to know that there is nothing a man should fear than himself. Better be friends with your enemies if you want to live forever. There are advantages. Loads but that is not the purpose of the report. The Beasts are people who have the will, the guts, and the resources to play God. How the world will change and move away from these defensive economies and stop wasting resources on wars is not our concern. We know how mankind will move away from defensive economies.

i] We shall reduce two-thirds of all people on earth, two-thirds of all animals once and for all. We shall send seven angels each with a cycle of slaughtering people.

ii] How this is to be achieved is through the Beasts II who shall mark everyone with a sign. Giving them marks on the forehead and right hand. Technology shall help us tag each one and give everyone serial numbers disguised as medical records. The rich or poor, tall or short, men or women, the young or the old everyone shall bear the mark of the beast.

iii] There shall never be weapons again as we know them today. The Beast II shall be responsible for making highly sophisticated

Weapons of Mass Destruction. [WMDs] that will help achieve the murdering of two-thirds of the population. That is the only way mankind will see no need to wage wars. Countries shall be left empty with plenty of land. These WMDs shall be in the form as Medically Implanted-Remotely Operated-Devices [MIRODs] which are to be distributed to unsuspecting billions.

Iv] The Pre-New World Order members will be responsible for the search of resources to enable such a technology. Therefore, whenever they mentioned the threat of WMDs to justify war they are telling the people the main reasons for waging the wars. To make WMDs as part of the New World Order. Something that was prophesied 2000 years ago and something that MUST be fulfilled. These acts are beyond mankind. The New World Order has started already. All men who have eaten the fruit of wisdom shall do this to eat the fruit of longevity. This is not a fruit that will make you live forever as we know that's impossible. Therefore, this means that your help and be part of this cult will be guaranteed. You being one of the few third that will be spared to start a new life. This is just like in the bible in the time of Noah where a flood killed most of the people. This is for real. People are taking advantage of the bible to make WMDs in broad daylight. People today are making these WMDs going everywhere to collect resources to make these WMDs. Waging wars for something they believe to be an obligation as more countries become friends. The more the world becomes peaceful and still making weapons, spending money on weapons when there are no wars will be the greatest threat to mankind's existence. Hence the New World Order [NWO] is there to take over during the transition phase. Mankind's stupidity will make him keep on spending on the military despite peace in the world. What he should do as peace prevails is to move away from defensive economies and find ways of expanding resources to accommodate the growing pressure posed by the population growth. The NWO is now responsible for the killing right now they are in the process of making and testing these WMDs. People are correct to worry about these WMDs. We have seen wars waged as far back as the 1960s for fear of these WMDs. These WMDs are being made by the Beasts II the same people pretending to fear their existence.

All the financial collapses are collections of money for making these WMDs. The world is being robbed. All banks emptied and money collected in broad daylight in order to make WMDs to be used on all of you. These guys don't sleep. They are going to war to get resources for making WMDs. The only question is what are you going to be part of a third of the population that will be spared. A cult exists today so secretive that you don't know what it does. You simply find money disappearing, and no one complains simply because mankind will only bring his own destruction if left to run things. You find most leaders being accused of not in control. Their policies are contradictory. They provide the best medical and living standards, yet they are afraid to starts wars but spend huge budgets on defense and the military. Such a combination of policies is not only dangerous but can't be left to go ahead. The cult led by the Beasts stepped in to safeguard the existence of humanity by killing two-thirds of the population using WMDs.

[Fictional scenario]

"Hey George, what do you think you are doing?"

"Doing my best providing the best medical, the best living standards at the same time making peace with everyone. I MUST not follow in the footsteps of my father going to war. I will go to church and I pray for our country. I am going to stop any unnecessary waste, but our military becomes first the best in the world you know what we are going to increase our budget to build more missiles and planes."

The second Beasts II stepped in.

"Hey hang in there. That's a combination of disaster. That can trigger a world war one day something we don't want. It's either you maintain peace but reduce spending on the military to compensate for the increase in the population and living standards."

"No, you know defense and the military are our priority. No can't do."

"Okay so create some enemies to justify the high defense budget."

"No can't do either. I can't start wars we have had that a lot."

"George, you are not being fair so who will do the killing?"

"I thought the Beast was now the one responsible for all the killings? My hands are clean and should remain like that."

"The Beast can't do that because we don't have enough money to do that."

"How can we when all your budget is military?"

"Sorry can't do. We are in the New World Order now until the president of the New World Order steps out I have nothing to do with the killings. Sorry."

George boastfully left the office. The Beast II stood there cursing like it's no man's business.

The next day George is horrified to find out his own people have been killed he cursed enraged.

"Killing is not part of my job description I am still not going to war."

He gets his missiles and attacks the mountains. After two years he was still refusing to go to war. Then his best of the best, the seven are taken in the Columbia space shuttle.

"Just like the seven angels in Revelations 13 who shall open the seals so that they pour their wrath on earth. We must invade and topple Saddam. We need the oil and money for the WMDs too so that in the future you will not be responsible for any killings. A New World Order."

"I will go but just this and the last time. Presidents are like gods too. Let the Beast be responsible for the killing and balancing of nature."

Collection of Money by the Pre-New World Order.

The financial worse of the past years were collections of money by the Beasts to prepare for the time in the bible when mankind will be forced to move away from defensive economies and create heavens on earth where networking and cooperation will be paramount. Just like those who fund drug dealers or terrorist we are funding indirectly those making WMDs to use on us as population control. As wars cease and nations become friends (look at the USA and North Korea) the fact that mankind is still spending trillions on stupid weapons can indicate a system that is poised to collapse. The fear among the New World Order circles is the fact that if unchecked this will trigger a sudden and fast world war that might result in the extinction of mankind. The population will continue to grow without the supporting infrastructure and resources while we continue to build nuclear weapons as well for that matter. One friction will cause the extinction of mankind. Hence the need for finding other ways of killing at a massive scale. Welcome to the world of WMDs. The threat is that are you prepared to let the Beast II to be responsible for playing God? For the killing of two-thirds of the world population? We know there is proof that some are making vaccines that will cause 99% of the population to die after a certain period. This is true. These people believe that it is not God but the early man who foresaw this using science that if unchecked mankind will become his own enemy. I think there is no need for WMDs if we can act now and change our mindset and move away from defensive economies. Trust me there are no aliens who will come and attack us. We will end up killing each other unless resources are used to alleviate pressure by finding alternatives. No need to kill two-thirds. Is it surprising that the so-called New World Order members are very learned people most with degrees and former leaders and leading businessmen and women? Most are part of a university club where views are shared, and debates are taken and solutions to problems are drafted and documented but kept in secrecy? It's nothing to do with whether you believe in God or not. It's up to all humanity to act now. Will you let the Beast II robe all banks in order to make WMDs which they are going to use on you? Or fight the Beast II today stop him and change. Move away from defensive economies gradually reducing weapons, etc.?

Food for thought: False Sense of Security.

The idea throughout this book is that a foreign nation in the form of the Beast II forced protection in that it created a situation that exposed the weakness of a country and then provided solutions to the problem it has created. It then goes on to put demands in return for its protection. So, it's like blackmail. It created the problem itself then prescribed a solution. But is this real protection or what has been referred to as grooming. More precisely, it's like being on death row. Being groomed to be killed. Given a false sense of security then killed when you least expected. Look at the JFK case. He spoke about enemies within. Even the day he died he talked about the threat of being shot. He knew someone had pretended to give him protection. Then exploited him. Parading him all over before executing him when he least suspected. This is a very common tactic, in fact, it goes back to the Tyburn era in England. Those about to be hanged were asked to wear their best before being paraded. They were asked to put on a show and not to show fear but to die in-style one might say. Just like in the Rome era with the execution of Christians. They were paraded and a lot of people would attend and those with money paying for VIP seats. In England, in Tyburn, this was a way for the councils to raise funds. This is true even years after as in 1629. When King Charles I had been tried for treason and found guilty, he was told that he would be executed. The day before the execution he asked for two shirts and the reason being that he did not want people to see him shivering because of the cold in case the people have mistaken it for fear. I explained throughout the volumes I & II that the Beast II is working very hard marking people with marks and digital serial numbers and advanced tools as revealed in Revelations. We know animals like dogs and cats are now given tags for identification and electric collars for controlling them and guiding them as a form of protection. They give people a false sense of security because it's not protection it's grooming as someone on death row and in the end just surprise you. The Beast II's job with the help of the dragon who causes fire everywhere is to kill as many people as he can. Human rights and the years of enlightenment has hindered the Beast II's progress in imitating God.

A common trick I have discovered is something President Eisenhower did during the late 1950s. We know there was a 10-year contingency plan already, and he wanted to start a war with the Soviet Union. We know he had two bases established in Pakistan, one of which was to launch flights for real into the Soviet Union and the other just for a decoy. We know too that he had two jet fighters. One pilot for actual secret flights and the other just for a decoy.

CHAPTER EIGHT

9/11 As Simply A Terrorist Attack.
Since Volume I, I have tried to be as subjective as I can, looking at facts and debunking all the conspiracy theories, one after another. In this chapter, I am going to analyze the role of the terrorists and in this the attacks as the ends in themselves. This means the terrorists had no other motive monetary, strategic, or with the aim to corner anyone to make them one's protectorate. The terrorists attacked simply because that's what they do.

US Law definition of Terrorism.

"Premeditated, politically motivated violence perpetrated against noncombatant targets by sub-national groups or clandestine agents, usually intended to influence an audience," [U.S. Code Title 22 Chapter 38]
US Law International terrorism
Regarded as acts that violate federal or state laws that;
i] intimidate or coerce a civilian population
ii] use intimidation and coercion to influence government policy
iii] uses assassinations and mass destruction to change government conduct.
Terrorism.
"is, in the broadest sense, the use of intentionally indiscriminate violence as a means to create terror among masses of people; or fear to achieve a religious or political aim." [Wikipedia]
UN definition
"terrorism as any act "intended to cause death or serious bodily

harm to civilians or non-combatants with the purpose of intimidating a population or compelling a government or an international organization to do or abstain from doing any act"
[Secretary General of the United Nations]
There are so many definitions of terrorism to suit different conditions and looking at different factors as to the reasons for carrying out a terrorist act. But one thing is for sure terrorism has no justification whatsoever though it is generally believed that this topic can be subjective as one man's terrorist can be another man's freedom fighter. Some tend to accept that in certain situations as a form of defense terrorist acts can be viewed as morally acceptable only if;
"a nation or community faces the extreme threat of complete destruction and the only way it can preserve itself is by intentionally targeting non-combatants, then it is morally entitled to do so,"
[Michael Walzer]
It is widely believed that the motives of the 9/11 attackers were to draw their concerns to international attention. Religion is central to their causes.

Background.

It is widely believed that Al Qaeda was responsible for the four coordinated attacks on the USA on 11 September 2001 killing 2996 and injury many. First, I have tried throughout the report to look at the facts and then arrive at a conclusion rather than look at the situation and ask why. I will make my own judgment at the very end of the report. This is possibly the trickiest part of the report because people's reasons especially associated with terrorism might not be logically proved or scientifically tested as I have managed to do with the rest of the conspiracy issues raised. Nevertheless, the truth will always prevail. 19 terrorists associated with Al Qaeda committed the 9/11 attacks. 15 of the terrorists came from Saudi Arabia, 2 from the United Arab Emirates. One from Egypt and the other one from Lebanon. The terrorists were grouped into four groups each group led by a pilot trained terrorist. The other men were for overpowering the pilots and crew. Two planes struck the two towers one in each causing the collapse of the twin towers. There were other separate incidents with another plane hitting the pentagon. The fourth plane crashed into a field in Shanksville, Pennsylvania after the passengers fought. The attacks brought America to a standstill and fear spread all over the country and worldwide as billions watched.

I think it is important here to note that:
"9/11 is the single deadliest terrorist attack in human history and the single deadliest incident for firefighters and law enforcement and law enforcement officers in the history of the United States, with 343 and 72 killed, respectively." [Wikipedia]
The US government did not hesitate and quickly listed Al Qaeda as the main suspect immediately calling for the extradition of Osama Bin Laden. The Taliban refused, and the US invaded Afghanistan. Osama Bin Laden initially denied responsibility. In 2004 he then admitted full responsibility.

Why Al Qaeda Straight away?

Al Qaeda had attacked the USS Cole guided-missile destroyer on 12 October 2000 in Yemen. 17 sailors were killed. Al Qaeda accepted responsibility. Sudan was held accountable by the courts and as a result, its frozen assets were then given to the families of the 17 killed and this was $13 million.

Why Sudan?

Sudan has been accused of helping and funding the terrorists Al Qaeda and as a result of their activities, 17 American sailors were killed. The families of the deceased sailors then sued Sudan sending court papers to Sudan's embassy in Washington instead of the Foreign Office in Sudan. Sudan had deposited its assets in the USA before the incident. After the incident when Sudan did not respond the courts awarded the victims' families more than US$300 million. The courts then froze Sudan's assets and requested the banks to handover Sudan's assets in America's banks.

The USS Cole Incident.

The USS Cole stopped in Aden to refuel when it was attacked on 12 October 2000. Two suicide bombers in a small fiberglass boat with C4 explosives exploded on the side of the USS Cole. This created a 40by 60-foot (12x18m) hole. It is believed that C4 explosives were used as a shaped charged.

Shaped Charges.

"This is a concave metal hemisphere or cone with a high explosive in a steel or metal casing. When the high explosive is detonated, the metal liner is compressed and squeezed forward, forming a jet whose tip may travel as fast as 10 kilometers per second. [Wikipedia]

A shaped charge with a metal liner is known to penetrate the armor of ships made of metal to depths of 7 to 10 times the diameter of the charge. The jet's shaped charge utilizes the kinetic functions of the charge rather than the heat aspects.

Munroe/Monroe or Neumann effect.

"is the focusing of blast energy by a hollow or void cut on a surface of an explosive." [Wikipedia]

A German engineer [Franz Xaver Von Baader] discovered that the use of a conical space at the end of the blasting charge would reduce the need for gunpowder at the same time increasing the explosive nature of the charge. Using a high explosive other than gunpowder will create shock waves. This is how shaped-charge-warheads worked. {the bazooka] also known as High Explosive War Anti-Tanks.

The interesting thing to note here is that these high explosives anti-tanks are also used in explosive demolition involving building made of steel mainly for cutting through metal columns, pillars, beams and for boring holes. When they detonate, they perforate the metal casings?

Hydrodynamic penetration.

High-explosive-anti-tanks (heat) warheads.

These shaped charges utilized the Monroe effect to penetrate thick tank armor. Initially, warhead guns for perforation were used in oil drilling. The machine guns would be fired in order for oil drilling to begin. A Henry Mohaupt of Swiss original invented this perforating gun during World War II after patenting his shaped-charge warhead traveled to Britain and France to advertise the warheads and close a sale.

Hydraulic Fracturing of concrete in the World Trade Center.

The plane was used as a shaped charge to penetrate the World Trade Center and inject large amounts of jet fuel into the floors weakening then before being pulverized. The original shaped charges were filled with gunpowder and later with nitroglycerin. nitroglycerin is used in explosions and demolition as it is a good explosive. During the war, this was used as a military propellant. During World War I HM factory Grenta was the highest producer. It is one of the hottest detonating high explosives. It is also an oily liquid that may explode if subjected to the following heat. It is also smokeless as an explosion which makes it a secret explosive agent. The main uses are in hydraulic fracturing where it is used to sink into cement and floors.

In oil drilling and the development of the shape charged warheads and perforating guns.

Before oil drilling, the borehole had to be cemented first to trap the oil and to avoid the collapse of the oil well. That, in turn, required that the casing be perforated so that oil will flow into the borehole from the surrounding area.

Ira McCullough [US2349666A - Perforator gun with improved] invented the multi-bullet shot casting perforator that was used to perforate the casing.

Henry Mohaupt patented his shoulder-fired rocket-propelled grenade launcher in the USA. [US2947250A - Shaped charge assembly and gun] while working for Well Explosives Company in Fort Worth, Texas he developed the cone-shaped charge explosive to perforate oil drill casing.

The USS Cole Terrorist Attack background.

Three factors were of grave concern to the Congress.

i] The inadequacies of US protection against terrorists

ii] The gathering and use of intelligence about terrorists' activities in Yemen.

iii] Overall US's anti-terrorism policy.

It was noted that some security procedures were not allowed and that the attack could not have been prevented.

Force Protection Procedure.

This has four levels of protection

A. Lowest form of protection

B Better than A but not fully.

C Better than B but to fully

D The ultimate protection.

At the time of the attack, the USS Cole was on Bravo. The questions asked were what could be done to increase protection in Yemen and the Persian Gulf where ships must refuel and collect local goods? Does the US have enough ground intelligence collection in the Persian Gulf? Was there adequate coordination between all departments and the proper exchange of information?

Certain factors were of concern it might have seemed as if the US deliberately created conditions so that incidents occur maybe to justify war in the Persian Gulf. The first one:

i] Why the USA chose to refuel in Yemen from 1999 instead of from Djibouti where it has refueled for years without elimination of terrorist risks? Up to the day of the attack, no specific information was received regarding Yemen.

ii] Planning ahead and or anticipating new methods of a terrorist attack. True US has been attacked with truck-bombs. What are their maritime equivalent and air equivalent?

Truck bombs-land

Fiberglass boat- water

Airplane -Air.

iii] Protecting against threats posed by persons with legitimate access issues raised by relying on private foreign companies with access.

iv] Role of FBI in overseas investigations. I need to have an in-depth understanding of foreign countries.

v] Ensuring coordination of any retaliatory response.

Availability of appropriate and adequacy of appropriate retaliation channels.

a) US Embassy bombing in East Africa—US cruise missile attack Pharmaceutical factory in Sudan.

b) East African Embassy bombing---US retaliatory attacks in Afghanistan in 1998. It is believed that the attacks were linked to Bin Laden.

The greatest challenge faced by policymakers was the risk and fears of further attacks in response to US retaliatory strategies.

Posse Comitatus Act.

Congress through this Act has forbidden the use of the military for duties related to the civilian government.

"It restricts the armed forces from acting "as a posse comitatus or otherwise to execute the laws," except "in cases and under

circumstances expressly authorized by the Constitution or Act of
Congress."
[Wikipedia]
9/11 attacks prompted the use of military force to fight terrorism.
Congress through P.L. No. 107-40, 115 Stat. 224 (2001) authorized
the use of military force against the 9/11 attacks' terrorists. After
9/11 due to the Posse Comitatus Act the President needed
Congressional authorization to use military force against the
terrorists responsible for the 9/11 attacks and P.L. No. 107-40,
115 Stat. 224 (2001) granted such authorization through the
Authorization for Use of Military Force [AUMF]. The President can
use;
"necessary and appropriate force" against those whom he
determined "planned, authorized, committed or aided" the
September 11th attacks, or who harbored said, persons or
groups." [Wikipedia]
Some have raised concerns about such authorization as they
viewed this as a blank-check an unjust way of giving the President
too much power without debates because it is prone to abuse.
The AUMF gave authorization for the invasion of Afghanistan,
Djibouti, Iraq, Somalia, etc.

War-Contingency- Plans and the Posse Comitatus Act.

It seemed that before the 11 September attacks the Posse
Comitatus Act restricted the use of military force against terrorist
acts or justify going to war. In other words, without such horrific
events, Congress might not have given the President a blank
check that is an express authorization to do whatever he wants
and to invade any country with the approval of congress. One can
say that 9/11 made it possible and easy to get blanket permission
to wage wars without the need to debate such decisions with
Congress. The problems faced by former presidents was the fact
that a short- and long-term contingency plan existed but without
the express powers to carry out that plan. The president had to
seek permission to carry out any military invasion. The threat

posed by chemical and biological weapons of mass destruction alone was not enough to justify the use of military force. This is true also regarding the Eisenhower era. We know for a fact that a 10-years-contingency plan against the Soviet Union was drafted in 1949 for events that were believed to take place 8 years later. When the time arrived, the President had a plan without the necessary powers to implement that plan. This caused the employment of short cuts in the form of unacceptable behavior like spying hoping that something goes wrong that will invoke an authorization to justify going to war. The perceived presence of WMDs alone was not good enough to justify invading other countries. We saw Eisenhower resorting to desperate methods establishing secret bases in another country namely Pakistan the idea being that if the Soviet attacked Pakistan for spying as the planes would be leaving from Pakistan. Once the Soviet attacked Pakistan then the USA would intervene to protect a weaker country against a bully the Soviet Union. In the end, getting what they wanted. A war with the Soviet Union. It should be noted also that the threats of perceived or real surprise attacks were high especially after Pearl Harbor.

Authorization for the Use of Military Force. [AMUF]
"Preamble
Joint Resolution.
To authorize the use of United States Armed Forces against those responsible for the recent attacks launched against the United States.
Whereas, on September 11, 2001, acts of treacherous violence were committed against the United States and its citizens; and
Whereas, such acts render it both necessary and appropriate that the United States exercise its rights to self-defense and to protect United States citizens both at home and abroad; and
Whereas, in light of the threat to the national security and foreign policy of the United States posed by these grave acts of violence; and
Whereas, such acts continue to pose an unusual and

extraordinary threat to the national security and foreign policy of the United States; and whereas, the President has authority under the Constitution to act to deter and prevent acts of international terrorism against the United States: Now, therefore, be it Resolved by the Senate and House of Representatives of the United States of America in Congress assembled." [Wikipedia]. 9/11 paved the way for future wars and use of military force against any nation with the President needing to give Congress only 48 hours' notice something that was not possible before the 9/11 attacks. This AUMF has made it possible for the US military to be involved in national defense and this has the establishment of the NORTHCOM the US Northern Command that covers the US, Canada, Mexico and parts of the Caribbean. Its aim is to help civilian authorities in case of a terrorist attack.

The USS Cole Terrorist Attacks Analysis.

Al Qaeda was believed to be behind this attack. Two suicide bombers left a huge hole in the USS Cole. The USS Cole was rescued by the Royal Navy Type 23 frigate, HMS Marlborough. The responders were the US. Air Force Security Forces, Force Quick Reaction Force based at Prince Sultan Air Base, Saudi Arabia. After that, the Marine Corps Security Force Company soon arrived but not fast enough to prevent casualties. After that another backup in the form of reinforced by a U. S Marine platoon with the 1st Fleet Anti-terrorism Security Team Company (FAST), based out of Norfolk, Virginia.

The Investigations.

The FBI and NCIS went to Yemen to investigate. They experienced a hostile climate. People were calling for Jihad against the USA. After some delay, the CCTV footage is released from the harbor side near the point of attack. The moment the boat attacked the USS Cole was deleted. In 2007 a judge ruled that the Sudanese government was responsible for the attacks. Relatives of the victims of the USS Cole argued that the terrorist would not have carried out the attacks without the Sudanese government. They accused" Sudan's government of providing support, including money and training, that allowed AL-Qaeda to attack the destroyer while it was in the harbor of Aden, Yemen." [Wikipedia].

The Master minder.

Abd al- Rahim Al Nashiri was arrested and charged as the master minder of the attacks. He is a Yemen of Saudi Arabia descent. He was subjected to torture; waterboarding and other extended interrogation techniques. Tawfiq bin Attash regarded also as the master-minder was captured and sent to Guantanamo.

Rules of Engagement. Implied order of a stand-down call.

These are believed to be the main reason behind the stand down. The guards because of the Pentagon's rules of engagement did not fire at the small boat they had no idea that the boat was carrying explosives. It is believed that soon after the attack another small boat appeared, but Petty Officer on the USS was asked to turn the machine gun away from the other boat simply because of rules of engagement. Lack of accurate information about the involvement of Al Qaeda made the USA not take retaliative action for the attack suffered by USS Cole.
"By 21 December 2000, the CIA had made a preliminary judgment that Al Qaeda appeared to have supported the attack without a definitive conclusion." [Wikipedia]
It was believed that the decision to take retaliation action was solely the new President's role. George Bush. Condolence Rice at the time asserted that the President was working on a comprehensive plan against Al Qaeda instead of retaliatory separate events.

Countermeasures as a result of the USS Cole incident.

i] Random Anti-Terrorism Measures- random security procedure that can't be predicted

ii] Anti-Terrorism and Force Protection Warfare Center at Naval Amphibious Base their objective; develop sophisticated methods to deter terrorists.

iii] In 2004 death sentences for Abd al-Rahim al Nashiri and Jamal Al Badawi.

iv] New Maritime Force Protection Command established 2004.

I have covered the relevant background material relating to the background before 9/11 and I looked at if Al Qaeda attacked the US before 9/11.

What might have led the terrorists to plan and carry out the 9/11 attacks? The argument throughout the report is that it is difficult to come up with an objective justification for carrying out the attacks. But I will look in general first at the reasons for most terrorists' acts.

i] Freedom fighter. Feels oppressed and to leverage for power. There is no evidence that America was oppressing any of the terrorists or members from their country Yemen, or Saudi Arabia which some were descended of. At the time the USA had agreements with these governments for initiatives against terrorism. We know that even with Sudan the USA had cooperated and worked with the Sudanese government to tackle terrorism.

ii] Felt foreign country, in this case, the USA as trespassing. I can only infer from another incident that occurred in 2002 regarding the Maritime Jewel a double hull oil tanker near the same area of Aden Yemen where terrorists attacked the ship using a small-boat called a dingy and perforating the tanker and causing an oil spillage. The other terrorists accused the French-owned ship of trespassing. It is believed that Al Qaeda claimed responsibility. Interesting here is the fact that Abd al-Rahim al Nashiri the same man accused of masterminding the USS Cole is also accused of masterminding this attack. So, we have a general background of his concerns and a statement supposed to have been made by

Osama Bin Laden points to the reasons why they carried out the terrorist attacks. Osama Bin Laden issued a statement, which read:
By exploding the oil tanker in Yemen, the holy warriors hit the umbilical cord and lifeline of the crusader community, reminding the enemy of the heavy cost of blood and the gravity of losses they will pay as a price for their continued aggression on our community and looting of our wealth.

Two accusations to note Aggression behavior trespassing into sovereign waters and looting I can assume oil.

The way the USS Cole suffered damaged suggested that it was hit with a conical shape charged explosives used for perforation. I think the terrorists might have thought that the USS Cole was carrying oil. It makes sense that the intention of the terrorists was not to blow the whole ship up as they were in a small fiberglass boat called a dingy too. The conical shape explosives with C4 might have been hidden in the boat and or attached to the boat with the intention of perforating the ship to cause a leak. This was the case in the MJ Limburg incident. That could explain why the captain and officers did not react as the small-boat approached. Although they sighted rules of engagement as a reason for the stand-down.

One man's terrorist is another man's freedom fighter.

In the early years, Osama Bin Laden is portrayed as a holy man fighting to free his people from "the infidels the Americans,". His concern; America's aggression, trespassing and invading the Persian Gulf simply because the oil-rich nations had nationalized oil wells. We have the USA President Eisenhower declared that "nationalizing the canal was not the same as nationalizing oil wells. [which] exhaust a nation's resource. In that case, these people [just based on that] are right to defend what is theirs; the oil wells. Probably change starts with the USA's foreign policy.

Having said that, I think it is also interesting to know that the USA had done a lot to establish links and cooperation agreements with the governments of the countries concerned. It had agreements with Yemen, Saudi Arabia, and Sudan and more interesting to fight terrorists. It is clear too that the countries mentioned above themselves had the same problems as America posed by the terrorists. I think it is worth distinguishing between pirates and terrorists. That region is well known for pirates who attack ships and boats in that area for other reasons mostly economical and commercial rather than for religious purposes. This is true even years back. The British have experienced these pirates. I have looked at the Persian Gulf Residency by the British above. We see a similar situation, pirates sabotaging ships just like the issues faced by the USA. The only difference being that this was in the 1800s. It is interesting here that the British Raj let the pirate's attacks happen with the goal to move in and establish themselves and offer the Persian Gulf Protection from the pirates in exchange for residency and control to the oil wells. This leads the British to make protectorate agreements with most of the Persian Gulf nations. The protectorate's agreements made the British the sole protector against pirates and terrorists. The nations were to leave the terrorists and the pirates' problems to the British who were to deal with these through a comprehensive plan that dealt with the whole region. They were also to leave foreign relations in the hands of the British. Any dealings with another country was through the British.

Is there a conflict of interest or two bulls fighting for the same cattle?

A first look at this arrangement throws a bad picture of the arrangements in the Persian Gulf. History has it that the British formerly or after the fall of the Ottoman Empire controlled and owned the Persian Gulf Wells. That brings us to the 1956 Suez Canal incident. The reason why the British wanted back the canal was because of its strategic and commercial attractiveness to the

British. A short route to the oil-rich Persian Gulf. We also know that America in Eisenhower time probably lacked what the British might call foresight by calling the Suez Canal-saga a trivial matter. To the British, the canal was as good as the oil wells. Now years later we see America trying to muscle the British in turn-taking some stake. Does that ring a bell? The Anglo-Dutch wars. Britain with no money facing the plague and then the great fire of 1666 needed to take some Dutch's lucrative stakes. Was that what America was doing in the Persian Gulf? Could this explain why there were so many terrorist attacks against America's ships than the British? Or it was down to experience. The British had been around since 1600 and had experienced what America was experiencing now? Was it another Suez Canal strategy of going behind America's back and recruit the Israelites to attack Egypt so that they invade Egypt and make it a protectorate state with its own powers but with foreign affairs activities in the hands of the British? It looked like the USA was claiming to be the Superpower the protector of countries in the Persian Gulf but in doing that shooting itself in the leg leaving it prone to more attacks at home and abroad? It can be inferred that it would make sense to suggest that the British probably wanted to be the ones in charge of giving protection to the Persian Gulf countries against pirates and terrorists just like it did years back. This could make sense. Very often after the USA had suffered attacks the first one to the aid is the British. It could simply be because they are more experienced and have been around for a very long time. It is true also that the British still had a lot of agreements with all the countries concerned. It enjoyed very close relationships with Saudi Arabia through the Saudi Royals. Let's say if an implied protectorate agreement was still in place between most Persian Gulf nations and the British then the Americans according to this agreement were the pirates or the terrorists. The British had promised to protect the Saudi's and other nations from anyone this included America's aggression. In that case, the mishap America was facing was due to a lack of understanding of that relationship. What concerned me or worried everyone was the fact that if the USA was the Superpower of the world why it was one of the countries on earth to suffer the worst attacks one after the other? Was it sabotage? Who were the pirates here? Who were the terrorists here? It's not a question of having many counter-terrorism bodies scattered everywhere that are viewed as to protect one's citizens and assets. It can be simply down to the fact that you have two male lions in the same hood and surely that can only result in dirty tricks, sabotage, terrorist acts against each other and outsourcing to third parties. See the Suez Canal case in Volume I. We have two bulls and they all want to be the best in protecting the others and to be a Superpower in the world. It is true that America's act during the invasion of Egypt in 1956 humiliated the British at the same time the USA became the 'Superpower'. Note also that I have dealt in detail about the Superpower status as a status near to being called a God. As such the real Superpower is omnipotent, omniscience and omnipresence. America suffering such attacks cannot have that status. How can you protect others when you cannot protect yourself? How can you claim to be a Superpower when no one fears you? You have beggars slapping you in the face. Are you the godfather? Are you mafia? In the sense that you must be feared. Who here would see God assuming he existed on earth and slaps him? Who would see a lion and attacks it? I am not saying that just because America is not killing people that is why it is not feared; no. This has nothing to do with fear but with respect and honor. I know this topic is subjective. Terrorists are not scientist they don't follow certain rules. Therefore, I cannot say for sure as there could be so many other reasons behind their motives, but that is the purpose of this report to try to understand the events that left scars and a lot of unanswered questions.

Interesting is the fact that America is reliving Britain's past.

Coincidence of following a film script it is astonishing that what America is facing now Britain has faced the same situation hundreds of years ago. I must note that the British have a system of recording all the events that occurred as far as the 1000s while America doesn't have the same privilege. These Persian Gulf incidences which America was facing, the British had experienced these before. In fact, everything that happened to the USA has been tried and documented by a man called Christopher Wren born in 1632 and died in 1723. It seemed whatever he wrote, did, experimented on and invented was adopted and implemented by Larry Silverstein, owner of the World Trade Center. Reading his life and works paints an astonishing picture that leaves a lot to be said.

CHAPTER NINE

Is someone behind all this?

The strong relationship between America and Britain does it involve this arrangement? In volume I, I have gone to extra lengths to explain the godfather-protege relationship, the master-student, the inner lookout post-outer lookout post in great detail. Is it what is happening here? It is just unbelievable to be a coincidence. I explained also how the map and layout of London, especially of 1666 and Newyork, are similar. It is official that London is a sister city of London. Striking here is the fact that this Christopher Wren redesigned the city of London after the great fire of London. The plan designed by this Christopher Wren of the city of London was not used after the great fire as far as we know, although it was similar to the original design it seemed though as the plan used to build Newyork. This Christopher Wren's ideas, works, research, investigations, you name it had a major impact and influence on what has happened to the USA since the year 2000 or even earlier. Notable

i] 1653 at All Souls College Oxford England

Christopher Wren designed an octagonal transparent beehive; a man-made container for keeping bees for scientific observations.

* USA 2002 Equivalent Guantanamo Cage set up by the US. A transparent mesh wire cage for Muslims; as an experiment for observation in order to replace white sugar with English honey?

>Octagonal like the Islamic Temple Mount or Dome of the Mount "initially completed in 691 CE at the order of Umayyad Caliph Abd al-Malik "[Wikipedia]

> For scientific observations of the bees

> For holding male bees indefinitely to see the effect of colony collapse disorder [CCD] same the USA under Bush were doing even the same using humans at Guantanamo.
>The USA is now adopting and testing British ideas indirectly. These ideas were first tested 349 years ago? To make things worse that same year in North America, Virginia in 1653 was the first-year slavery was introduced and acknowledged by the courts in Anthony Johnson v Robert Parker. It is the first time the courts acknowledged that a free black man can keep another black man as a slave. We see after Bush Barack Obama instead of correcting history lacked the guts to correct history and close the camp. Whatever their reason it is in line with Christopher Wren's beehive, the same person who might have influenced Hitler with the Auschwitz camps. This Christopher Wren experimented with medicine as well as injecting fluids into the bloodstream of dogs. Now we see the Americans doing the same and constructing the concentration camps. Maybe we invade Cuba just like what happened to Germany for them to shut down Guantanamo Bay. If they can't listen maybe, we ought to go there and force them to. Have you not learned from Auschwitz? People steal British crooked Ideas look at the World Trade Center Towers it is based on this beehive by Christopher Wren developed in 1654; a death trap of a building initially designed for insects, not humans. The same year the courts in North America first approved slavery. What does he go on to do next? Kill Osama Bin Laden together with his son? Can two wrongs make something right? The idea was to capture and put him on trial. It took a lot of time and planning to correct and make history right and all these people you are putting in power are weak they just go with the flow? What a waste. Given an opportunity to correct a past wrong and for approval rates we are back in 1653. In the case of JFK Oswald was to go through the justice system and be tried and then hanged. At least he had been treated fairly. Look what happened to Jack Ruby after killing Oswald. He ended up in jail. The American justice system takes a lot of shortcuts. Innocent until

proven guilty. You will see that another event will happen so that America tries someone justly without anyone taking the law into their own hands and slaughter each other. The attacks they are facing are in direct response to their legal system. Wake up people inferior thinking everywhere. We are still thinking just like we did 2000 years ago?

>Christopher Wren then started to observe the moon, and he helped in the invention of the telescope. He then moved to architecture and redesigned the St Paul's Cathedral and the city of London before and after the fire. He started experimenting with what he learned at the Royal Society.

> He changed the tower of the cathedral with a doom.

>He used gunpowder to demolition the St Paul's cathedral as an experiment through digging a box hole and blowing up the building.

> 3,6 kg of gunpowder dismantled the building faster than he thought. The blast lifting 3000 tons up in the sky. The second time he was not there but the second blast was huge as 8kgs of gunpowder were used.

*Incomes Larry Silverstein is interested in very tall buildings and gets a lease for the twin towers. We see his desire to rebuild the World Trade Center complex.

>Somehow Larry's Silverstein towers are hit by two planes. Now gunpowder is replaced by the modern equivalent of thermite a combination of aluminum from the body of airplanes and iron oxide from the jet fuel. The towers were destroyed very fast and how many people were displaced to heaven? 2996 only four short to match Christopher Wren record the difference that the British scientist sent 3000 tons of rubble in the sky by using gunpowder and the American sends 2996 human lives to heaven assuming that he wanted the towers gone and someone did him a favor. As per our script; The Death Trap.

>We see this Christopher Wren facing problems of rejection, his ideas and plans facing rejection from people who didn't want to give up their land or title rights. We see him having issues getting insurance and or funding ending up resorting to threats. Telling

everyone that everything on earth belonged to the king as he was the king's surveyor. Using a verse from the bible from 1 Corinthians 10v26 and Psalms 24 that threatens people with death if they refuse to open the gates to their houses for the king probably the reason behind using gunpowder in case some get killed so he can just take the land easily.

>Still that period 1666 we see the king Charles I, who is in George Bush's situation having his father been the King and the President respectively and with low approval rates for both. We see other people who are loyal intervening to help lift them to their respective positions in power. We see the great fire of London in 1666 and the 9/11 fire that killed 2996 people.

>For both, money, is a problem missing $trillion and with the other; soldiers i.e. Royal Navy being paid in debt vouchers. After the fire and the twin towers attacks their problems evaporate. Both can rebuild, Bush's government tax lax to Larry, compensation, and insurance eases the problems.

>We see terrorism being of concern for both and that started the recording of foreigners' details and in Bush's time the application of Christopher Wren's ideas and we have the Guantanamo Cages. Colony collapse disorder experiments with racial connotations using Obama to justify a wrong playing of mind manipulating games.

>Again, remember the USA was implementing and testing the British ideas developed 349 years ago when slavery had just been introduced?

>What follows that? Calls for the presence of weapons of mass destruction. But who is making the WMDs? Or who is supposed to make the WMDs? They want oil to save money and use the money to make weapons of mass destruction. Dwight Eisenhower the USA President in 1956 said that he can only authorize a war only if a nation with oil reserves had nationalized oil which would otherwise exhaust their financial resources. Iraq nationalized oil wells in 1972.

>The calls for Weapons of Mass Destruction has nothing to do

with the fear of being attacked. No! It is in line with the fact that people worldwide are all becoming friends we have the USA and North Korea on talking and handshaking terms at the same time we are spending a trillion dollars on weapons instead of extra accommodation, better ways of doing things, infrastructure, etc. how are we going to maintain the imbalance. Many years ago, wars had corrective effects. The world had enemies now everyone is a friend. The real threat is that the population is going to keep on growing and we are going to keep making weapons and maintaining huge defense and military budgets. In the end, people will start to feel as life will become harder and harder and humanity will be tempted to start a war to reduce the pressure on land and resources but that will be it. The use of nuclear weapons and intense fighting will result in the extinction of humanity.

> So, the call for WMDs is a call to make the WMDs and all these people who think are part of the New World Order are secretly emptying our banks. The financial collapse is a daylight robbery to make weapons to kill at least two-thirds of the population. These people are making weapons of mass destruction and tagging everyone. Most of you don't know that but you are being programmed given secret medical devices but in reality, being fitted with bombs. Some are making vaccines that will eliminate 99% of the population.

> So, the calls for WMDs are calls to make the WMDs to be used to kill people as to correct population and resources imbalance. No wars and plenty of weapons are viewed by the few who think they are very clever (maybe I am one of them-joke) as a recipe for disaster. To save humanity they believe they must make WMDs which they will implant into all of you and selectively kill you.

> You, believe it or not, it is up to you. All I can say is that think outside the box. Above all, ask yourself this; If they are going to kill two-thirds of the population deliberately are you going to be part of the third that will be spared?

>,In the end, we seeking Charles I and President Bush who was accused of being incapable of running his administration at the pentagon now in the President's seat with high approval rates and

now all banks and financial institutions asking him for help. We see banks asking the President to bail them out, from his lowest point the Nadir to his highest the Zenith.

>Has someone been blackmailing him? Maybe someone offered him one of the so-called Protection. Slavery if you ask me. How can one kill others in order to offer them protection and lift them up high? Who decides who dies and why? This era people should belong to live on earth forever and never die. Dying for someone was a thing for the past when misconception was the norm of the day. People thought paradise or that phase in human development when people don't see differences. A time when there won't be any pain and troubles and all things bad was something for the afterlife. No. We must achieve that state here on earth. We are not moving as we should be in the development stages. We are still in the defensive stages when security and protection are important to us. We spend a lot of money on defense and security. When we have achieved that stage of understanding and development, we shall spend money on cooperation and networking. We shall strive to link the whole earth and travel the globe like what we do in a city. All boundaries will have gone. We shall never fear to be attacked because we will have developed an understanding that our worst enemies are our selves. There are no aliens or other creatures like dinosaurs that will come and eat us. We are all brothers and sisters. We shall live as we live in a house. No boundaries or seeing of differences. All the money we spend on defense and weapons we shall use it to link each other and maybe find alternatives for everything like fuel, energy, accommodation, food, etc. We will have developed that much that the gods will be jealous of us. God that is if you believe in God gave us everything and our own kingdom on earth, so we live like him and be like him. Honestly what he wants is to create small gods, us. Just with his image and with our own kingdom here on earth. It is a challenge. This paradise is something we must create here on earth. That is why I am saying that the first stage is to remove things that keep making us be like the early man of 2000 years ago. Fearful of dinosaurs building walls and fences and huge fortified houses when

what we should be doing is not bothered about all that. People steal or rob because they are hungry or don't have money or something because your leaders just the day before that wrote a blank check for an advanced missile. If that money had been plowed back in the economy, this man would not have thought of stealing. When we have achieved that understanding we will sleep in the open. No worry about too many things. We shall never be jealous about someone's possession or wife or husband we shall everything we need that you shall not want someone else. People, now they run to God. They think heaven or paradise is up there? They kill themselves and run to heaven committing suicide to be in paradise? Its incorrect heaven is here on earth. Paradise is here on earth. It's the stage of development that will make us reach a heavenly stage. This applies too to all mankind whether you believe in God or not. God tested mankind. Do you want to be like me and become a god here on earth with your own kingdom or you would come back to me to my heaven? Mankind is fighting to die so that he goes to God's heaven when he has given you the opportunity to be your own god here on earth by developing or evolving. God is a spirit. Heaven is on earth. Heaven is what we make it. We need to develop to live to heaven standards but here on earth. Stop wasting resources on weapons to kill each other but aim to start creating heaven on earth. Heaven is a place where everyone is free and your brother or sister. That is without boundaries. Networking, cooperation, and communication. Highly advanced transport system, etc.

CHAPTER TEN

Attacks on the Pentagon.
The use of conical-shaped charged high explosives like the
bazooka in the form of a plane or just a missile?
Please, I ask you to take a quick look at a photo of the attacked
USS Cole on 12 October 2000 search on Google. Look at the
damaged part of the ship. A high explosive conical shaped charge
was used with C4 as the inside explosive to perforate the ship
within short distances but with massive impact that left a gushing
hole. It is an advanced technology that manipulated physics and
hydrodynamics applying all these into the day-to-day terrorists'
activities with such horrific results. Plane or no plane that
attacked the pentagon first I am saying it is advanced knowledge
and use of advanced technology. If you know that a bazooka can
do the same damage, then you will know that it might not have
been a plane. If it was a plane, it could have been fitted with one
of these. I have a question for all of you. We know that the first
thing George W Bush did after 2996 Americans were killed was to
go and attack people who live in the mountains. True? The
methods used, and the stealthiest do not go hand in hand with
what we are witnessing. How many scientists in America and the
whole world? How many conspiracy theories we have and how
many are believed even up to today? I ask you another question.
Can the caveman be capable of doing something even you
yourself can't understand or prove? I am saying that the methods
used are so complicated and very advanced that the best of the
best can't understand how it is possible for towers to fall that way
and how things happened the way they did? Still even now 17
years later a lot of things are still a mystery. Surely can the

caveman carry out such attacks without assistance from advanced educated people? We know for sure Bush went to attack the mountains of Afghanistan. Even though Iraq was the target from day one due to the presence of contingency plans and the nationalization of oil wells by Saddam Hussein it took the Columbia space shuttle disaster for Bush to invade Iraq. Once he invaded Iraq it all became clear to everyone what really had happened. Even if we are agreeing that it was the terrorist's ideas who acted alone the methods, they used to be believed to be advanced methods that can only point to the fact that someone else too advanced as well might have given them a hand somehow. A conical shaped charge is very powerful as it is based on the hydrodynamic principles that a conical shaped-charge can perforate steel and metal bodies. The original ones were used in the drilling of oil. It was used to bow rocks or to perforate the metal casing before drilling oil. What is surprising is that somehow the attacks are similar or looked like they continued from the last attack? In 2000 a conical shaped charge explosive like a bazooka was used to perforate the USS Cole ship. In 2001 the terrorists used the same method to attack the pentagon. Rules of engagement were cited as the reason behind a stand down stance. When the USS Cole was attacked, the investigators could not get the CCTV footage prompt and when they did, the footage showed that at the time of the explosion the scene was deleted. In 2001 when the video was requested, they delayed too and when they finally received the tape the scene when the explosion happened was deleted too. Then you are left with questions. The first attack was a drill of the things to come? Is someone offering USA protection in the form of guidance and tutoring? Do we have two Superpowers competing? Or is this sabotage and blackmail? To understand this, I think it is fitting to look at the level of power and tactics employed and whether the players involved are symmetrical or asymmetrical and the implications.

Asymmetrical the US has a professional army that employs certain rules and procedures whereas their opponents employ unconventional methods to gain an advantage. Most of the

casualties being suffered by the USA are due to this setting. This is true as the US and all its personnel must observe certain rules and regulations in its operations. This is true when it comes to rules of engagement the main reason attributed to the causality suffered in the USS Cole incident. I believe also that this played a major part in the Pentagon attacks. The resources are a total of different scales with the US with huge ships carrying several personnel whereas their opponents here the Al Qaeda with little dingy boats. The inability of the USA to defend itself properly is due to this setting that it is not suited to deal with this kind of insurgents that used guerrilla tactics. This was true in the USS Cole incident. Al Qaeda with a small boat resorted to the use of advanced technology attaching not just a C4 but what I believe to be a shaped-charge high explosive missile in front or underneath the boat with the resultant explosion. It's not just an explosion, but a carefully planned attack that utility physics, mechanics and hydrodynamic knowledge that the mechanical space in the underneath kitchen of the ship acted like a chamber for thrust generated by the blast that helped lift the USS Cole up killing 17 crew members. What is surprising here is the fact that AL Qaeda is portrayed as uneducated people who live in the mountains, yet all their attacks leave the most educated cream of Americans without answers but a lot of questions? Take the 9/11 attacks, how the towers collapsed? How they stealthily achieved hijacking 4 airplanes without being stopped. Their methods are advanced to such an extent that you start to think that someone very intelligent is behind them? No doubt the US did not underestimate them and respondent by commissioning the Predator drone an unmanned drone used for surveillance and attacks as well. The use of unmanned methods in response to suicide terrorists. For example, according to Wikipedia;
"On 3 November 2002, the CIA fired an AGM-114 Hellfire missile from a Predator UAV at a vehicle in Yemen carrying Au Ali-Harith, a suspected planner of the bombing plot. Also, in the vehicle was Ahmed Hijazi terrorist.) U.S. citizen. Both were killed."

CHAPTER ELEVEN

Impact of terrorism.
I tried to give an unbiased account derived simply by analyzing the facts and all the information I had, nevertheless this time I think it is time to list what I think are the real culprits behind these terrorists.
[Has this ever been into your mind? Osama Bin Laden's father was in the construction industry with a wealth of $7 billion. Could this have necessitated or triggered the rise of Al Qaeda? It seems all that they do is to destroy very prestigious buildings and embassies. If the family was in the construction industry isn't this a nexus? For-hire fast demolition agents?]

Protection and Protectorate.

First, I think by now you have come to understand that a few countries offer protection just like a gang leader would give you. The same protection just like the one the mafia's godfather would give you. This protection is based on the fact that you are required to do what they call initiation. This begins with them giving you a task so brutal that doing it would guarantee your acceptance. Refusal can result in rejection or being framed and killed because after that you are regarded as knowing too much. This initiation is like insurance to them that you will not tell their activities to outsiders. This initiation can be something beyond your wildest dreams. In most cases, it involves taking another life. Once you accomplish that they can give you protection. If you don't do what they have asked you; to them, you are out. Another way when you can get this protection is when you have valuable resources like oil. In this case, protection is given to tackle your external threats like piracy and terrorism. The protector then let you be responsible for internal affairs while they deal with the external factors. In addition, there is a clause that the protector will also demand to deal with any of your foreign relations. In some cases, foreign nations must go through the protector in order to deal with you. Anyone wants to make deals with you must be referred to the protector. In this way, the protector does not ask a lot from you only that they have access or favorable oil deals in return. The protector normally does not deal with the issue of piracy and terrorism as individual cases. Instead, the protector adopts a holistic approach to dealing with all the problems of piracy and terrorism. In most cases, the same protector provides protection for several nations in that region, in the end, the same protector would be responsible for the whole region. The protector's goal is simply commercial in nature and for strategic advantage to some extent.

Analysis of the 9/11 hijackers.

A quote from Wikipedia best describes the 9/11 attackers;
"The hijackers in the September 11 attacks were 19 men affiliated with al-Qaeda. 15 of the 19 were citizens of Saudi Arabia, and the others were from the United Arab Emirates (2), Egypt, and Lebanon. [1] The hijackers were organized into four teams, each led by a pilot-trained hijacker with three or four "muscle hijackers," who were trained to help subdue the pilots, passengers, and crew." Wikipedia.
To further analyze this, I think it will be beneficial to put the information in a table below. It's clear all men are believed to be members of Al Qaeda. Al Qaeda is believed to have been formed by Osama Bin Laden who was a Saudi Arabian citizen born to a rich multi-millionaire father whose business was in construction. During the 1979 Soviet Union's occupation of Afghanistan, some Mujahideen declared a holy jihad war against the Soviet soldiers

and among them was this Osama Bin Laden. After the Soviet Union's withdrawal, Al Qaeda as the liberator of Afghanistan remained and established bases there. It must also be understood that Saudi Arabia is a rich country with large oil reserves, but its involvement is due to the religious beliefs they have. A 1973 warrior named Wahhabi believed that the country was gifted with oil so that it helps other nations. So, the table below gives nationality and the number of hijackers from that country.
See the table below.
(continued)
Nationality
Total Hijackers
Number
Value/Year
Saudi Arabia
19
15
1915
United Arab Emirates
19
2
1917
Egypt
19
1
1914
Lebanon
19
1
1914

I noticed that this is like a coded message. Out of curiosity, I ended up with years. 19 hijackers 15 from Saudi Arabia. I got 1915 then checked what happened in 1915 to Saudi Arabia that might explain this. Surprisingly just like I have been arguing in the first volume and in this Volume to has been supported beyond doubt.

1915 Saudi Arabia. The treaty of Darin 1915.

In 1915 the United Kingdom signed a Protectorate agreement with the ruler of Najd called Abdul-Aziz ibn Abdul Rahman Saud who went on to form Saudi Arabia as we know it today. The treaty made the House of Saudi a British Protectorate meaning that Britain would be responsible for its protection from external threats that included pirates and terrorists. The question that comes to mind straight away is the fact that was America seen or viewed as such by Saudi Arabia. A pirate or a terrorist? I think for now let's get to the basic facts first. This king agreed to enter the war as an ally of Britain against the Ottoman Empire. We know for sure that the Ottoman Empire was destroyed, was America now the New Ottoman Empire? According to Wikipedia;
"The Treaty was the first to give international recognition to the fledgling Saudi state. Also, for the first time in Najd's history, the concept of negotiated borders had been introduced. [4] Additionally, the British aim was to secure its Persian Gulf protectorates, but the treaty had the unintended consequence of legitimizing Saudi control in the adjacent areas. [4] The Treaty was superseded by the Treaty of Jeddah (1927)" [Wikipedia]. An interesting point also to note here is the fact that somehow the word Darin is associated with assisted suicide in the fact that the people regarded as daring are people who would go to extremes. The word dare is derived from the word dare which means to challenge or defy to prove courage or loyalty. Don't forget the Saudi and the British are rooted in the notion of the monarchy where men and women die for the monarchy.

The United Arab Emirates as the Trucial States including 1917. General Maritime Treaty of 1820.

Trucial States; this was a British protectorate from 1820 to 1971. This included a lot of Persian Gulf nations that included the United Arab Emirates. The General Maritime Treaty was a treat between

the seven states of the United Arab Emirates including the other nations. The treaty was made to stop the plunder and piracy by land and sea. The treaty prohibited piracy in the Gulf banned slavery and required all usable ships to be registered with the British forces and to display red and white flags. These flags remain even today. The treaty was a British strategic plan to exclude other powers especially European countries like Russia and France and other nations like the USA. This treaty was important because it gave rise to the formation of what is called the United Arab Emirates on 2 December 1971 and through other treaties. A number of treaties followed the General Maritime treaty namely the Perpetual Maritime Truce.
Perpetual Maritime Truce.
Perpetuity meaning;
"refers to an infinite amount of time i.e. lasting forever."
This treaty prohibited any acts of aggression. This also gave protection to the telegraph line and its stations. There was a plan for the treatment of the debtors who absconded without paying this came into effect in June 1879. Just like the original, it dealt with piracy. Britain aimed to influence the rulers of the Persian Gulf. Through other treaties, Britain expanded its military and political powers within the Persian Gulf.

Egypt 1914. The Sultanate of Egypt.

Okay, then I went to check what I can get for Egypt in 1914. In November 1914 the British declared war with the Ottoman Empire and Egypt was part of this empire and Britain signed a treaty making Egypt its Protectorate. Before 1914 the British had what was called a veiled protectorate. That means Britain had no formal protection agreement but just a de facto over the country. In 1914 the British removed the khedive from power and replaced him with their own puppet a family member too.

Lebanon.

I then went to check Lebanon. In November 1914 the British made the Ottoman Empire its protectorate and the Ottoman Empire included what is now known as Lebanon. So, it was a protectorate when it was under the Najd as the Ottoman Empire.

It is clear from the above analysis that Britain was the undoubted power and protector of the Persian Gulf countries from 1914 to 1956 and after that most of the nation's got their independence even then still Britain had ties with these nations acting as an overseer responsible for putting its puppet even after their independence. Britain as the sole protector of the Persian Gulf States was never challenged during these times by either the states or other powers. A clear pattern can be seen. All the countries concerned were all at one-point British Protectorates. We also know that the nations signed a perpetuity contract that was changed over time. Although this means nothing without knowing what the USA did to invoke attacks by these terrorists. The USS Cole and the MJ Limburg incidents highlighted what the remaining terrorists thought about the USA. The USS Cole was perforated with a shaped charge high explosive on the side with the aim of causing an oil leak. The incident killed 17 soldiers. The MJ Limburg was perforated as well, and the main reasons are that they were accused of stealing the oil that is piracy and mainly trespassing into someone's territory.

Looking at the treaty we can ask a few questions.

I] How is America viewed in this setting by the former Persian Gulf States. It is clear that America is viewed with suspicion. It is believed to be looting the Persian Gulf Oil and is regarded as a pirate. This is evidenced by the attacks in Yemen. The USS Cole. It's just not the USA but other foreign nations as well including France evidenced by attacks on the MJ Limburg in Aden Yemen. The ship was perforated by a dingy carrying a sophisticated shape charge high explosion missile attached. Even though Al Qaeda are cavemen, their methods incorporate advanced ideas in mechanics and physics utilizing the knowledge of hydrodynamics and other physics principles. That can also point to a foreign hand. The fact that British ships in the area are not considered as hostile and in fact are not attacked points to the indirect existence of the perpetuity Protectorate relationship. The British are viewed somehow as still having some form of control over the Persian Gulf states. It is a fact that they provided weapons and finance as far back as 1820.

Saudi Arabia's stance as innocent and its justification.
It is clear that the British signed different treaties for protection with the Persian Gulf States. I have mentioned the above treaties namely;
I] The Darin treaty 1915 Saudi Arabia-Britain
ii] The Sultanate of Egypt of 1914
iii] The General Maritime Treaty 1820 and the Perpetual Maritime Treaty that covered UAE and Lebanon and other Trucial States.

Outsourcing of Protection by the Persian Gulf.

These treaties even after independence existed informally as the British continued to play a key role and establishing special relationships with these former states. Britain removed accountability responsibilities from these states the moment it declared that it will protect these states and therefore answerable to whatever these states are accused of. In a way, the Persian Gulf States outsourced protection from the British. Like I said above the protectorate treaties made it that any foreigners wanting to deal with the protected nations had to go via the British. Any oil deals were referred to as the British first. The protected states would be responsible for their internal affairs and all the external affairs including dealing with pirates and terrorists was up to the British. This setting left a loophole that can be taken by the protected states where they can commit an attack and channel responsibility to the British. I understand that the families of the victims of 9/11 launched a court case under the Justice Against Sponsors of Terrorism Act requesting the Saudi government to pay for sponsoring the terrorist. If the protectorate treaty were still in existence, then such court cases might fail because the Saudi government can easily deny responsibility simply because any dealings regarding terrorists and pirates are dealt with by the British. In such a case a court case can succeed if also directed at the protector, in this case, the British.

Protection offered by Britain to the Persian Gulf as a blanket immunity. An automatic exemption.

Britain's offering of protection to Persian Gulf states gives these nations an automatic exemption and in turn encourages these nations to actual sponsor terrorists knowing that they can get away with it. Even though these treaties ended after independence a special relationship still exists. In this light, it can only be inferred that such a setting exists even today. That could explain why British ships are not attacked in the Persian Gulf. To understand this in more detail, I think let's look at the kinds of protection offered by these treaties. The Perpetual Treaty established a permanent treaty at sea. That is a forever contract implied or not with the British. The sheiks promised to cease any attacks of British ships and this remains the case even today. That highlights that somehow the treaties or just the understanding still exists.

A look at the treat illustrated that;

"The Exclusive Agreements of 1892 made it obligatory for the Trucial Sheikhs not to enter into any agreements or correspondence with any power other than the British Government. In return, the British took the responsibility of defending the emirates states from foreign aggression. The Exclusive Agreements represented the final tier in the treaty structure created by Britain in the Gulf in the 19th century and continued to be the cornerstone of British domination in the Gulf up to their withdrawal from the area in 1971." [Wikipedia].

Other countries like Germany, France, and Russia challenged the British's stance of making the Persian Gulf a 'British Lake'. The Anglo-American treaty of 1944 acknowledges that Persian and Saudi Arabia oil belonged to the British and the treaty made the two Superpowers share Iraq and Kuwait oil. By 1956 America's grip on the middle east had grown significantly.

"The Suez Crisis of 1956 marked the demise of British power and its gradual replacement by the USA as the dominant power in the Middle East." [Wikipedia].

The big question to ask is this; did the same settings existed in the late 1990s and early 2000s? And what impact could that have had? Is it also surprising that all the terrorists are from countries that once were British Protectorates? All are from countries with a monarchy. These countries torture people in broad daylight in the name of the monarchy. Monarchies have existed for centuries. Most have been around on or off since the 1600s. If we look at human rights at this time, we can see that it's the time when people had no rights at all. Slavery was just being introduced across the globe. Today less has changed most monarchies rules dating back to the 1600s are still in place and active. When it comes to human rights and the rule of law, we can see that a lot has changed in recent years. Recently within 100 years, a lot has changed yet still in countries with monarchy torture is done and authorized by the monarchies themselves. This is true in England even though torture is not permitted the monarchy can nevertheless authorize torture. In this case, there is an implied authorization to those concerned as long as it is viewed as necessary to protect the monarchy people use torture secretly and is still common in Britain. Of all the people the British have not changed much since 1605. The thinking is still the same as in 1600. In 1605 the king ordered the torture of Fawkes also known as John Johnson in the Tower of London.

"'If he will not other wayes confessed, the gentler tortours are to be the first usid unto him... God speed youre goode worke. James." The King's words [Wikipedia.] This Fawkes is caught and on 8 November after the authorization of torture by a monarchy he is tortured and on the 9th he confessed. The fact why I am looking at Britain is mainly because the Protectorate treaties declared that the protected nations had no worry about issues of piracy and terrorism as these were outsourced for the British to deal with. All the countries with active terrorism today were once British Protectorates. I have shown you beyond doubt that the ideas and examples are derived from British history. Someone behind all this has knowledge of the British practices and history and the way of doing things. We have seen all the works of a British astronomer, physicist, scientist and architect named Christopher Wren born 1632 influencing everything from the methods of attacks, dealing with the terrorists which are putting them in a transparent cage-like in Guantanamo bay, and use of his methods to control the population. He wrote a manual on how to do it. We see his ideas and experiments now being applied in real life at a cost to human life. The British assuming, they are behind this are Clever. They tested with bees in 1654 and in 2001 they let America experience the same with humans. In 1666 this Christopher Wren experimented with buildings lifting up 3000 rubble into the sky and in 2001 we find nearly 3000 people being lifted to heaven. It is clear from the facts presented that the twin towers were death traps. Someone with the detailed knowledge of the buildings was behind this or was the master-minder. The person knew that if the planes impacted exactly at the points, they impacted no one would leave the building. The idea was to match exactly the number dead, or the amount of rubble lifted up when Christopher Wren experimented with gunpowder to demolition a building.

The Mirror-Image notion.

London and Newyork are officially sister cities. I have explained how this came about in Volume I. Newyork's plan is a mirror-image of London in 1666. I have shown in Volume I that somehow either the city officials or someone wants Newyork to experience

what London experienced. Or they are using the experience of London from 1666 and apply this to Newyork to solve Newyork's problems. It can't be a coincidence. These are my reasons why it can't be a coincidence.
The map of London 1666 which was used to design and develop Newyork as I said was and could have been the one designed by Christopher Wren.

Christopher Wren as a pioneer of Newyork City.

It would make sense if the map redesigned by Christopher Wren was the one used to develop Newyork. After the fire of 1666, we know as I pointed out that this Christopher Wren as the King's surveyor redesigned a map of London when the fire was still destroying the city something he had desired before evidenced by the fact that he declared that he wanted to make London as beautiful as other cities. He had just been to France, Paris. When he came back, he realized that London, as compared to other cities, was like a slum. He designed a map of London and this map or the original blueprint was used to develop the city of Newyork. This could explain why Newyork employed a lot of his ideas and designs. What is shocking here is the fact that what happened on 9/11 and the surrounding area explains names on the London map? Are you lost? I know it's so unbelievably true that it's unbelievable. It's like someone used 9/11 events to describe places and names of places on the map of London in 1666.

Mirror Image Map of London to what happened on 9/11.

i] Eastcheap. This was a meat market in the city of London in the 1600s after the fire. Streets were lined with blood and meat parts that were in the butcher's stalls lining the streets. On 9/11 the streets on the side of the towers where the people fell to their deaths was that same street on the map of London referred to as the Eastcheap Meat Market. On 9/11 we saw people lying on the ground. The streets had limbs of humans scattered everywhere and were bloodied too. We also know that the terrorists are from the East and they could have been employed to exert a cost the cheap way in case of a misunderstanding. Let us assume that Newyork officials are refusing to pay royalties for using blueprint plans to construct Newyork when the original plans belonged to the British. In reality, the British also stole the ideas from Jerusalem; maybe the reason why the Newyork officials are refusing to pay royalties for the plans and ideas. In that case, the Eastcheap can be used to sabotage things seen as equivalent to the number of royalties they are refusing to pay.

ii Falstaff's Boar's Head Inn on a map of London.

The equivalent of this place is also near the twin towers in the area below the towers. The street next to the towers where the people on 9/11 fell hitting the head first on the pavement simply because the head weighs more around five kilograms. We now know because of the Falling Man that some people fell to their deaths. The equivalent of this area on a map of London was called the Falstaff Boar Head Inn.

Iii] The Royal Exchange on the 1666 map of London was trapezoidal, with an open area plan. This was the focal point of commerce where traders gathered in the middle. In the 1666s the market was used by Lloyd's Market which was a syndicate of insurance traders and buyers. On the Newyork map, this was equivalent to the World Trade Center Building 7. This also had a trapezoidal floor plan. The place had an open floor plan. This could explain also why the WTC7 building free-fall. The Royal Exchange was associated with the idea of a Timeball in later years. This was used to determine the exact time. The ball was dropped from the roof of a building using the Timeball mechanism. The Freefall time was kept a secret by the city officials and for a fee, they would tell the captains the correct time. These captains needed to know if their clocks were correct this was after the 1850s. Somehow also the World Trade Center Building 7 freefall like a time-ball.

Iv] Christopher Wren's model of a beehive is the same plan used for the World Trade Center Building with three zones and see-through rib vaulting and flying buttresses columns. Wren's plan had three zones, with a single express elevator than goes from the ground floor to the highest level. The other lifts took people to the next levels. On the next level, there were other lifts that take people to the top zone. There were lifts within the zones and two floors linked with express lifts. Only one set of lifts that took people to all three levels. Yes, the plan was perfect for bees that could fly out if on top-level imagining that a fire broke out but for people, this was a death trap. The building was built of glass throughout. Just like the World Trade Center which had the open column see-through plan of rib vaulting and buttresses column with glasses in between the 'ribs'. Wren discovered a great idea. The bees never made honey in the third zone. That also can be viewed as a lesson for the perfect height of these buildings in case of an emergency like a fire. It sounded as well as if someone was saying where the planes struck are the maximum permitted levels of which the building's height should be. Anything above is incorrect an issue addressed in the building standards.

V] Christopher Wren's experiments with the gunpowder to demolition the St Paul's church could this have been the basis of the 9/11 attacks methods used? Wren carried out the first blast using 3,6 kg of gunpowder. The second demolition was carried out when he was not there. I can only assume that since the first blast had destroyed the building, it was not enough to do real damage. That meant a need to increase the amount of gunpowder to be used. Wren knew that could result in damage to the building or even death of people surrounding. He was the King's surveyor and therefore any damage will be attributed to the king and as such he decided to leave knowing that his deputy will carry out the demolition using 8kgs of gunpowder. This, as expected, caused a lot of damage. Come 9/11 we see the planes used to demolition the buildings whether as a terrorist's incident or not we see the same impact.

It seemed everything happening in Newyork at the time was based on the previous work of this Christopher Wren. In his life we know he ended up experimenting in medicine injecting fluids in the bloodstream of dogs. His observational studies with bees led to the creation of the Guantanamo Bay. What is the real intention of the government regarding Guantanamo Bay? I am sure also that Christopher Wren's ideas are the same used in the Auschwitz. The theme is the same we know the Nazis ended up experimenting injection fluids into the bloodstreams of the Jews just like this Christopher Wren doing the same with dogs. Let us hope that America learns a lesson and close the Guantanamo Bay Cages.

The interesting thing to note is the fact that Christopher had experience with the issues regarding the difficulties of implementing plans. It was not a straightforward process as he witnessed. People who owned the buildings in the city had refused the compensation deals he had offered them on behalf of the King as not enough. The people wanted high compensation for their land and buildings. The king had no money, so Christopher Wren's frustration was later seen and evidenced by the inscription that was later found on the buildings he had redesigned after the fire. The Royal exchange one of his work and it had the bible inscription that;

"The earth is the LORD's and everything on it."

The meaning has been explained above. This was like a threat that reminded the people of the powers of the King. Him from a bishop's family and representing the king knew that the people needed to be reminded that if you disobey, you would be lifted to heaven. It was a threat as well in that the bible King David had written the Psalms threatening the people with death if they refused to open for his son King Solomon. The question to ask here is that did Larry Silverstein had difficulties in destroying and redesigning the building?

Why the Port Authority of Newyork leased the Twin Towers in the first place?

My arguments in Volume I are the fact that the towers no matter how beautiful they were had been made obsolete. The system was based on the obsolete idea. The towers were old at the time. The towers were built at the time when rules and regulations tolerated materials like asbestos and lead. The floors had encapsulated asbestos that at the time of the lease was supposed to be removed. The Port Authority had to take off the asbestos and this would have cost them around a $billion that alone is the value of the buildings. Occupants rates were low as the buildings were old and very expensive to run in terms of lighting and electricity. Demolition of the building was going to cost the Port Authority a fortune. The only feasible plan was to lease the Twin Towers. We know Wren was very eager to experiment with gunpowder to reduce the cost of demolition and the time it took. Did Larry Silverstein had the same ideas or advised as such?

Larry Silverstein A Protectorate?

The idea of protection is common in Europe, especially in England. The country offers you protection and as a protectorate, you must be given a mark of some sort? Twitching or a reptile-looking eye or something. That shows that you are one of them. In return, the Beast II works very hard to offer you cheap ways of doing things. In return, you offer lives and blood. It's a give and takes the situation. Protectorate or protection can be express or implied. So how did they do it if it was a protection?

The people who offer protection or protectorate status have been there for centuries and doing the same thing. Over the years they have developed a network of people that they almost control the world. They have their own people everywhere. They rely on identification through GPS. That can only mean that the subject that needs protection must have had an appoint at a special hospital to be given an implanted chip that can be linked to GPS. A lot of studies over the years have made it possible to utilize science and manipulate them here to make real things in the world that can be used to command and direct people. Science has made it possible to move a muscle of a frog using just salt. Imagine the development of electromagnetic studies. That can only mean that now electrical impulses can be used to make human beings' muscle twitch as a way of giving secret commands. Then on top of that picture drones flying all over the area through a remote-controlled device. Imagine now all the technological development grouped together. We have a human commanded remotely operated via an implanted device and hence protection. Now remotely a coordinated team can give commands to people remotely just by poking them or causing their muscles to twitch. Let's say you want the subject to turn left you simply make the muscle in the left leg twitch. The subject will simply turn left. Now imagine the development of dog collars years ago. A certain amount of electricity can be induced to give commands. We all know and probably used a dog collar as kids in the lab at school. Now imagine that technology combined with the above advancement I have already noted. Now the subject can be commanded and directed using the twitching of muscles like frogs in a lab. On top of that secret electric collars through the implanted device can be used to zap an electric impulse maybe on legs to indicate a stop or a no, or a duck or a jump command. Then through the art of hypnosis we now have software and technology that can be used to give commands when a person is in deep sleep and that person understanding the message and when he wakes up, he might be remembering what is said. Add this technology to our subject. Now somehow, we can even interrogate the subject in his sleep. Then comes the neurological studies and MRI technology that can easily map and image the brain. With this kind of technology now we can tell when interrogating our subject in his or her sleep to find out the way he was feeling at the time when we asked questions and whether he is telling the truth or lying. We can now tell if he is upset or happy. Now put all the technology together. Now we have a chance to give commands in dreams that can still be remembered as dreams when a person wakes up. Now we can communicate when a person is asleep. We can give commands as well. That does not stop there. Technology has made it possible to hear what is very far by recording and amplifying. Sounds happenings in a surrounding radius can now be heard and recorded. Likewise, the opposite is true. We can reduce the volume so that a person can hear only the sounds very close to himself or herself or simply insert the sound into his eardrums at low levels but enough for him or her to hear that message. Now we can tell our subject something in front of everyone but only our subject can hear that message. Then in recent years a way of making digital-like tastes have been developed. Now people can feel what another person is feeling. Somehow in delayed-time-manipulation and the time-delay continuum theory in physics a person can now feel what another person is feeling. We add all this to our subject now we can command our subject with easy. He feels like his hand is on fire instantly he knows what that means. Now using all this technology, we start teaching our subject to communicate without talking with his mouth. Hey, can this technology be abused?

The rise of the modern highly advanced terrorists disguised as a protected subject.

Looking at all the 9/11 terrorists they all had some problems with them that required some form of protection. These people are also regarded as lawbreakers. We have seen this since the Roman times that those criminals in jails would be given a task in which they would die anyway but die free carrying out a task than die in prison. It is true also that countries that offer this kind of protection do not usually have the death penalty. This is not a coincidence; no. It's a fact that these countries don't have a death penalty in that it is not formal, but you are given a task to carry out in which you will die too. So, this kind of protection requires that a person has committed some kind of crime to justify being protected. It is no wonder also that everyone ends up on protection. The whole system has things in place to make sure you can't have anything normally it's either you have a lot of money to get a basic need or you must go through the illegal road. Also, to note here is that not all technology is beneficial. Some of this technology is there to change a normal man and leave him with the brain of a toddler. Torture is prevalent and yet disguised. Very sophisticated hacking and torturing tools are used. Normal people are tortured so that they end up as protected maybe suffered brain damage or something. In most cases, these countries have a power like a monarchy that gives blanket protection to whoever tortures on their behalf. The institutions are there to set up people as a way of protecting the monarchy. These countries have eugenic policies as well and are not tolerant of foreigners who are regarded automatically as terrorists anyway to give their protection system an alibi. The monarchy rarely denounces torture because they believe to preserve their way of life, they must torture people. Normal people are tortured to the breaking point so that they are recruited as terrorists or end up doing evil crimes. In Volume I, I have shown how this is common in Britain. Years back people were offered a chance to die in style after committing crimes or even wrongly accused. They were paraded in the streets before being shot. So, in short, this protection can be to protect you only in the case of people who are rich with money. The other group of people is that of people who are regarded as "criminals" even if not guilty. These are tortured to breaking point and told to commit crimes as a way out of the pain. Hence the rise of the advanced modern-day terrorists. Most are viewed as on death-row.

Command center.

Today's terrorists are not cheap people but are chip people. They have marked most of them. Uneven eyesight; look at Mohammed Atta. One eye is like a reptile on the side a Mark of the Beast II in Revelations 13V 1-18.
The other three Wail al Shehri, Waleed al Shehri, and Satam al-

Suqami all had been subjected to severe mental stress with one of the brothers have complained about that. All three had been exposed to the traumas of being tortured or witnessing such a situation. This can also explain the fact that they were protected directly or indirectly. Tortured to the breaking point until they agree to kill others as a way of easing pain and as a way out. Satam al Suqami had been married to a young girl as an arranged marriage and then blackmailed after that. It is true that this is a kind of protection. That even though the marriage can stand those offering to keep an eye on him might use that to try to incite him to become a terrorist. In other words, he is tricked so that he cooperates. So far, all five of the terrorists who hijacked American Airlines Flight 11 qualified for this protection and if they did, we can also assume that they might have been part of this implied secret Protectorate treaty.

Who did benefit from the attacks first economically and then the impact of lost lives?

Every decision taken by a financial institution a bank etc. is to make a profit and financial gain. The pentagon just a day before the attacks had $2,3 trillion missing. The policies taken by the federal reserve the (third type errors) set the ball rolling and passed the debt to the consumers by taking the little they had as savings. In the end, the government was better off after 8 years with banks now needing a bailout. What the government did was to send a rolling ball or stone collecting all the money in the economy stealing from consumers who are given a false sense of security by purchasing homes they can't afford. At the end of the 8 years, they had been working towards the house and suddenly, they are in a difficult situation they lose their jobs they can't afford to repay the loan. They fail to pay the repayments after getting a bank loan towards the house. Income dwindled after the recession as they lost everything to include their jobs. The houses are then taken back, and they are now in a worse off position. Now it's reverse. A quote from Wikipedia sums it all;

"Falling prices also resulted in homes worth less than the mortgage loan, providing the lender with a financial incentive to enter foreclosure. [clarification needed] The ongoing foreclosure epidemic that began in late 2006 in the US and only reduced to historical levels in early 2014 [51] drained significant wealth from consumers, losing up to $4.2 trillion in wealth from home equity. Defaults and losses on other loan types also increased significantly as the crisis expanded from the housing market to other parts of the economy. Total losses are estimated in the trillions of US dollars globally." [Wikipedia.]

The point here is the fact that okay, the terrorists destroyed the Twin Towers, but they were part of a wider team with the goal of making financial gains and alleviating their problems.

Throughout Volume I, I have argued that the ideas behind the buildings originally were based on the semaphore system something that started in the 1850s even earlier in England. I have shown also that the idea of the timetable which the WTC7 building was based on started in England. The plans used to build Newyork were to some extent designed by an English man from Britain called Christopher Wren or that they used the original plan which Wren used to redesign the city of London. Nevertheless, everything I said in this Volume has somehow origins in England or have roots in England. The Great Fire of London was used as a case study in order to solve the problems at hand before the 9/11 attacks. Everything seems to have originated in England. I know America was under the British that could also explain why everything now seems to be derived from the British. Americans are half English and they share a lot in terms of customary laws and ancestry. The main idea behind this Volume is the fact that I said that 9/11 was not just a terrorist attack but a cold and calculated way of making whoever was behind this very rich in the long run. A prediction tool. 9/11 attacks were a means to an end instead of an end in itself.

9/11 Attacks as a trigger of the 2008 crash.

The 9/11 first as I have shown in this Volume was meant first to reverse the government Blackhole. Money was in the economy and federal measures used for ball-rolling the loss from the government to consumers. In the end, we saw a powerful President and begging consumers and banks. But could this be the real reason behind all this? The answer must consider also the fact that there was a 2996 lives price tag. No one in their sound mind would kill at such a scale just for ball-rolling the missing $trillion. It makes no sense, and this exonerates the government. In other words, the question is; who benefited the most? We know what happened on 9/11 was something that tried to destroy records, transactions and damaging the nerves of the financial records. But people don't make money by hiding or destroying records. So how? The only way that makes sense is through some form of prediction and stock dealings. So, the fact is who made a lot of money than anyone else for the ten years after the 9/11 attacks and why? If 9/11 is carried out to help its people get better through a lot of ways which I will mention later. We now know the collapse of the economy happened in 2008. See also calculations under cycloid. Okay without pointing fingers the task was to look at who among everyone had done very well when everyone else was not and why? After finding who did very well the first question to check was whether they had dealings with anyone who was in the World Trade Center Buildings. Any of the investment banks situated within all the towers. Then look at who and how they dealt before and after the 9/11 attacks. Research has shown that;

Only the UK had recovered very quickly and seemed not to have been affected like the other countries. Bear in mind that a lot of factors come into play too and because of that, we shall proceed very smoothly.
"The number of millionaires in the UK has shot up by 41% over the past five years, with one in 65 adults now classed as having a seven-figure fortune thanks to booming house prices and stock market gains."

The Guardian Thu 27 Aug 2015.

What is interesting here is the fact that some of this is attributed to booming house prices and "stock market gains" but caution should be taken not just to conclude based on that fact? Lottery winnings, population movement, etc., business deals, etc. should be taken into account as well but overall booming house prices and stock markets seem to be the main money-making strategies. Bear in mind that soon after the 9/11 attacks people were very afraid and insecure as they witnessed the destruction of the twin towers. I also highlighted the wrong or third type errors federal laws adopted and the incentives that targeted the housing market that resulted in the subprime housing loans. These were bundled and passed to other institutions especially the UK. They were sold in the UK cheaper than their actual values that in the end contributed to the housing market economy.

"Britain's billionaires have seen their net worth more than double since the recession, with the richest 1,000 families now controlling a total of £547bn.

Their assets have increased from £258bn in 2009, a rise of more than 112%, according to the 2015 Sunday Times Rich List. The past 12 months saw the biggest bounce for the UK super-rich in six years, and London now has 80 billionaires, up from 72 last year more than any other world city."

The guardian Sun 26 April 2015.

Again, this could be due to many things again we shall proceed very slowly.

"The collective wealth of Britain's richest people has more than doubled in the last 10 years, according to the Sunday Times Rich List.

The figure has more than doubled since a total of just under £250bn was recorded in 2005, despite the world economy being gripped by a punishing recession over much of the last decade."

The Guardian Sun 26 April 2015.

"Britain is the only country in the G7 [could be because it's not in

the euro] group of leading economies where inequality has increased this century, according to a report published on Tuesday…
The increase in inequality has coincided with a boom in the number of rich and super-rich people in Britain. There are now 44-dollar billionaires in Britain, compared with eight at the start of the century, while the number of people whose net worth is at least $50m (£31m) almost quadrupled to 4,660." The Guardian 14 Oct 2014
I have relied on The Guardian newspapers even though the same articles appear somewhere else.
This without a clear analysis might be misleading. First, I think now it's time to establish the nexus. The real link between those investment banks whose records were destroyed by the 9/11 attacks their practices and the link with the countries that did very well. To understand these, I will list all the investment banks and institutions based in the world trade center. I am not bothered about the airlines involved. My argument is that anyone to benefit must have direct links with investment institutions physically situated in the destroyed towers. These investments could not be expected to reproduce the records assuming that all their offices were in that building without backups. So, who was in the World Trade Center?
World Trade Center Building 1,2,7
Salomon Smith Barney
37 Offices in World Trade Center Building 7 Dominated took 37 out of 47 offices.
Financial Institutions
WTC7
Morgan Stanley
31 Investment,
Marsh & McLennan Companies
8 Floors
Hartford Financial Services Group
3, Financial Institutions
American Express Bank International

Financial Institutions
Provident Financial Management
2 floors, Financial Institutions
Standard Chartered Bank
4, Financial Institutions
Lehman Brothers
Investment,
Continental Insurance Company
Reinsurance
Anthem Blue Cross and Blue
Investment,
Oppenheimer Funds
Investment,
Guy Carpenter
Reinsurance
Garban Intercapital,
Investment,
Keefe, Bruyette & Woods
Investment,
AON Corporation
Reinsurance

A quick look at the above Investments companies in all the World Trade Center Buildings it is straightforward that Salomon Smith Barney by far occupied a lot of floors and it is the only one that occupied building 7 only. Salomon Smith Barney [SSB] from now occupied 37 of the 47 floors in the World Trade Center Building 7. This is the only building relevant to the report. I have shown from the first Volume that the idea behind these towers was something that has roots in the semaphore system and the time-ball. All this originated in England. The time-ball was a way of telling the correct time. A ball was dropped to tell the exact time. This was needed by the ship captain whose clock would lose a few seconds over time. This information was a way of raising money for the city authorities as they would ask for a fee. The time was kept as a secret. The same idea as I have highlighted could be used to predict the time the ball would fall that is the time the economy

would crash. It also gets interesting in that World Trade Center Building 7 is the equivalent to the Royal Exchange in London. The idea behind this exchange was to act as the central center of commerce and above all, it housed Lloyd's Insurance Market which is an insurance and reinsurance market. The Lloyd's Insurance is a syndicate and not a market. The Lloyd's probably is the only company of this type. It's a collection of millionaires and others who come together as a group and bet on insurance buying and selling shares this way. A syndicate is a collection of people playing as a group to make money. The role of the syndicate is to pool and spread risk. In 2017 the assets of the chain were more than $50billion money that could be used by the syndicate. This syndicate deals with insurance of a variety of things.
Okay back to the need to establish the nexus. The company with so many offices and documents in one building that ended up being demolished somehow will have an alibi of not producing documents if requested to and in the future can mislead others and end up in dodgy deals.
Did Salomon had deals with the UK or other countries? We know that the UK defied the economic recession and came out smiling after ruling out some factors like migration to the country, lottery winnings, business deals, etc.? The main things that will be of interest are the extraordinary gains in houses and stock market.

The Nexus Salomon Smith Barney.

"Salomon Smith Barney, the investment banking arm of Citigroup, the giant American financial services group, has become Britain's top adviser on mergers and acquisitions. It advised on 35 deals worth £37.1bn in the past 12 months, according to Dealogic, the research group. Salomon, which was ranked fifth in 2001, advised on some of the biggest British deals, including the Government's £7.6bn de facto takeover of Railtrack, Royal Dutch/Shell's £4.3bn acquisition of Enterprise Oil and the battle for P&O Princess Cruises.

However, the value of the deals in Solomon's table-topping performance was almost 20 percent lower than that achieved by Dresdner Kleinwort Wasserstein in 2001, when DKW advised on 38 deals worth £46bn ($64.9bn). In 2002, UK mergers and acquisitions were worth £157.2bn, a fall of 68 percent on the boom year of 2000." The Telegraph 29 December 2002.

A year after the 2001 crash we have Salomon Smith Barney topping up the list of the best investment advisers. First, before saying a lot we need to look at its dealings leading to the 9/11 attacks or just after. A quote from Impact Law gives us an insight into the reputation and dealings of Salomon Smith Barney.
"The firm was accused of intentionally giving false stock ratings during the telecom bust in an effort to lure and keep investment banking clients. The securities fraud investigation against Salomon Smith Barney began in 2002 under Eliot Spitzer, New York's Attorney General, and ended in April 2003 in a $400 million settlement." [Impact Law]
The remainder is food for thought for the reader. Only you can answer all the questions. I have given you the background story, the facts, and the judgment the answers are up to you.

ABOUT CAROLINADEIVID

We are everywhere bookstores, online shops, and social media simply search for Carolinadeivid or Touchladybirdlucky Studio.

OUR BOOKS

The Vice President The Electronic Transfer Series (2 Book Series)

The Vice President The Electronic Transfer (2 Jan 2019)

by Carolinadeivid

The Vice President The Electronic Transfer: Volume II: The Death Trap (24 Jan 2019)

by Carolinadeivid